SOCIALISM
My Part in its Downfall

NEIL CULLAN McKINLAY

Unless otherwise indicated, quotations of Bible verses are from The Holy Bible, The New King James Version © 1982, Thomas Nelson Inc. Nashville.

Published by WEEMAC Publishing

July 2026

CONTENTS

SOCIALISM: My Part in its Downfall

The further society drifts from the truth, the more it will hate those who speak it.
George Orwell

Preface

Unlike Spike Milligan's book, Adolf Hitler: My Part in His Downfall, my SOCIALISM: My Part in its Downfall is not meant to be a humorous book. Sure, you may find some sections funny (whether intended or unintended!). However, the intention of this book is to be a serious reflection on the modern state of affairs. Okay, I will try hard not to be too serious all of the time, and I promise to inject some (of what I call) humour into what follows.

Socialism is now very much unashamedly out of the closet, (if it ever was in the closet). At its base, Socialism is all about wealth redistribution by government. If this sounds to you like what you think government is supposed to do, then this book is intended to help you think this concept through. What is government for? Is it there to protect the freedom of the individual? Or is it designed to look after the masses through a system of wealth redistribution?

America added a bill of rights to sit beside her constitution. Why? To protect the individual citizen from unlawful government interference in their lives. Socialistic governments increasingly expand as they implement more and more of their (wealth redistribution) social programs, and, as they do so, individual rights, i.e., basic freedoms for the individual, more and more decrease. Bigger government means greater taxes. Taxes are the reason why America came into being in the first place. A high tax burden creates angst among the people, and they become revolting.[1] Thus, the American Revolution in brief.

Socialism is not about the haves giving to the have nots. Rather than the individual "haves" cheerfully participating in the voluntarily (tax-free or tax-deductable!) giving of charitable donations, Socialism is about the government taking from these "haves" and redistributing their wealth to a society of its own creation, i.e., the entitlement society. Thus, Socialism is a self-perpetuating system of wealth redistribution. Instead of rolling up their collective sleeves to work hard and earn an honest crust, the people now look to the government expecting a handout. In Western democracies, one can either vote for freedom, or one can vote for free stuff.

What about the destitute and the disabled, those who are unable to work, those who are unable to find employment? Government welfare should be a last resort, and even then, it is not the role of governments to dole out other people's money, but simply to encourage charity in society. There is the way of Socialism, and then there is the Christian way. In the former, government is a major player. In the latter, government is merely the referee.

Private Insurance

Adolf Hitler: My Part in His Downfall was first written in 1971. I first read it in 1978 while languishing in the North York General Hospital, Toronto, Ontario with my first spontaneous-pneumo-thorax (collapsed

---

[1] Don't forget your sense of humour while reading this book!

lung) without any OHIP (Ontario Health Insurance Plan) coverage. Though Spike Milligan made me laugh (but only when I breathed!), post-surgery, I was almost daily visited by a person asking how I was going to pay for my lung operation and hospital stay. I was hospitalized for a whole month over the Christmas and new year period of 1978-79.

Having grown up in Scotland, and, having lived next door to the Vale of Leven Hospital, over the years I had been used to simply popping into the hospital with my various cuts, bashes and bruises (which were made worse when I had to start climbing over the gate into the hospital which they closed and locked at the top of my street on McColl Avenue). I think all I was ever asked for at the hospital was my name, address and religion. The NHS (National Health Service) never asked whether I had insurance, whether it was current, or what type of insurance I had, or did I have a Blue Cross or an OHIP card.

"Mr McKinlay, how are you going to pay your hospital bill?" they would ask me in North York General. That is one scary question! Especially when you have no money and no idea.

Socialized medicine is how they do it in the U.K. Your neighbours pay your hospital bills for you. Oh, and you help to pay theirs (if you are the type of person who likes to work, as in have a job, the more you earn, the more you pay). Fair? Socialists think so. But what's wrong with health insurance? "Not everyone can afford health insurance," says the Socialist. "Why should I be made to pay my neighbours' hospital bills, especially when they smoke two packs of cigarettes a day along with drinking a carton of regular coke which they mix with the gallons of rum they drink? No wonder they can't afford Health Insurance! They waste their money on drinking and gambling and who knows what else!" Anyway, I'm sure you're getting the picture.

So, should we have State and/or National Health or should we have Private Health? Australia has both Public and Private Health Insurance. I'll let you guess which of the two gives the better service. Why do you think that is? Why is it that even people from Australia, Scotland and Canada fly to America for specialist medical treatments? There's no public health system in the US. (We'll talk about Obamacare later.)

No one is saying that doctors and nurses and all the hosts of medical technicians and assistants don't work hard in public health systems. Of course they do. And most of them should be awarded medals for the way they love and care for their sick and injured fellow human beings. However, everyone knows that private medical health is better than public medical health. Admit it! But why is this? Surely it's because governments are useless at running businesses.

There's more to Socialism than socialized medical care. Much more. And that's the point. Socialism is a philosophy. Socialism is a world view. Socialism is a religion. Whatever Socialism is, know this: Socialism is not Christianity. Socialism is not a Christian philosophy or a Christian worldview. Nor is it a Christian religion. I'll try to demonstrate this and a whole lot more in the following.

This book covers things from Global Warming to what you and I can say or even think. Like something out of 20,000 Leagues Under the Sea,

Socialism gets its tentacles into every nook and cranny of your life.

As you read this book, keep in mind that the first to call their political opponent "Hitler" or "Nazi" loses the argument! And keep in mind that there are different shades of socialism. All socialism is shady. Ominous! So that you catch my drift, here's a wee sample of what I mean. Says David Van Gend,

> The soft socialists who command the high ground of our culture are different to their hard-edged forebears, but with genderless 'marriage' they will further a century-long quest to deconstruct the family and subject it to the state.[2]

Yes, there's more to Socialism than taxpayer funded health care. A whole lot more.

Spike Milligan was in hospital with a "bad back" caused by a slipped disk before the U.K. brought in the National Health Service on 5 July 1948. Says Milligan just as he was being called up for the army, (don't miss his humour),

> I was put in Lewisham General Hospital under observation. I think a nurse did it through a hole in the ceiling. Specialists seeking security in numbers came in bunches of four to examine me. They prodded me, then stepped back to see what happened. "He's still alive," said one.

---

2 David Van Gend, *Stealing from a Child: The Injustice of 'Marriage Equality'*, (Connor Court Publishing Party Ltd, 2016).

Then they hit me all over with rubber mallets and kept saying to each other, "what do you think?" Days later a card arrived saying "Renal Colic". The old man in the next bed leaned over and said in a hoarse voice, "Git aht of here son. I come in 'ere wiv vericose veins and they took me 'pendix aht." … Those sons of fun at the hospital, having failed to diagnose my ailment, discharged me with a letter recommending electrical treatment, and headed "To whom it may concern" – I suppose that meant me. It was now three months since my call-up. To celebrate I hid under the bed dressed as Florence Nightingale. [3]

How did I pay my hospital bill for my collapsed lung operation and hospital stay? I simply paid the OHIP payment I had missed when I was between jobs. Then my health insurance kicked in again and took care of the bills.

Private and personal insurance is a wonderful invention, be it for your health care, your travel, your car, your house, your death etc. It relieves the burden on your neighbour, i.e., the rest of society, to look after you. It does away with the need for the State to look after you through exorbitant taxation. It does away with the need for government expansion into every nook and cranny of your life. How so? Because it does help to do away with Socialism…

---

[3] Spike Milligan, *Adolf Hitler, My Part in His Downfall*, (Penguin Books, Kindle Edition, 2012).

Defining Socialism

Socialism. What is it? Is it a good thing? Is it a Christian thing? And if it's not, what is un-Christian about it? Isn't Socialism about helping the poor and the downtrodden of society? Isn't Socialism about countering greedy Capitalism and looking after the worker or the "battler" as societies' strugglers are called in Australia? Anyway, whatever it is, isn't Socialism at the very least more "Christian" than Capitalism?

It seems to me that there is a lot of confusion out there as to what Socialism actually is. There're different types of Socialism, though it's probably better to say that there are different shades or flavours of Socialism. No one admits to liking the Nazi type of Socialism. National Socialism didn't work out well for Germany and the rest of the world in WWII. And what about the type of National Socialism they have in China right now? Are these types of Socialism the same? Are these actually Socialism?

Is bankrupt Venezuela a Socialist nation? Cuba? Or are they Communist? What's the difference between Socialism and Communism anyway? Is there really such a thing as Democratic Socialism? Is Government taxation Socialism? Why is Socialism so hard to nail down and accurately define? Or is it?

It concerns me that Christians get tangled up in the red-tape of Socialism. The following was written by Tim Keller, a Christian minister,

> I know of a man from Mississippi who was a conservative Republican and a traditional Presbyterian. He visited the Scottish Highlands

and found the churches there as strict and as orthodox as he had hoped. No one so much as turned on a television on a Sunday. Everyone memorized catechisms and Scripture. But one day he discovered that the Scottish Christian friends he admired were (in his view) socialists. Their understanding of government economic policy and the state's responsibilities was by his lights very left-wing, yet also grounded in their Christian convictions. He returned to the United States not more politically liberal but, in his words, "humbled and chastened." He realized that thoughtful Christians, all trying to obey God's call, could reasonably appear at different places on the political spectrum, with loyalties to different political strategies.[4]

How were the American's "Scottish Christian friends" able to convince him that they were not the Socialists he had first thought they were? It doesn't say anywhere in the article how the "humbled and chastened" Christian man from Mississippi was convinced even though they had "loyalties to different political strategies." The article seems to infer that Socialism is taught in the Bible! What else are we to conclude? I don't know any Scot who would say that the present controlling political party (of the devolved government), i.e., the Scottish National Party, is anything other than Socialist.

---

[4] Timothy Keller, in an article *How Do Christians Fit Into the Two-Party System? They Don't*, Sept 29, 2018, Sunday Review, The New Your Times.

I grew up in Scotland. As it was then so it is today. Scotland is a *very* Socialistic country. I personally held to a Marxist type of Socialism – until I became a converted Christian in the late 80s while living in Canada (another very Socialistic country).

Let us now begin to define our terms. Whether cultural or economic, Marxism is still Marxism. And Marxism is simply Socialism by another name.

The Socialist wishes to influence society with Socialist ideas. If Socialism is simply Christianity by another name, then Christians wish to influence society too. However, though both support and advocate for social reform, Socialism is taught nowhere in the Bible.

It may help by using the word "Progressive" to denote those who advocate social reform, but only if we use the word *Progressive* to refer to those who hold a Socialist view as opposed to a Christian view of societal reform.

But here's where it gets really difficult. Both the Socialist and the Christian are happy for the Government to be involved in Social reform. But here's the difference. The Socialist is willing to hand over his/her freedom to the control of the State. Everything therefore belongs to the State to do with in accordance with its own flavour of Socialism. The Christian, on the other hand, believes that all things belong to God, including the State. Therefore, Socialism and Christianity part ways when it comes to ownership. Socialism does not believe in private property.

Joel McDurmon spells out for us what Socialism is,

Socialism is the belief that individual private property and free-markets are bad ideas. It is thus an anti-Christian and anti-biblical belief. Socialists believe that governments should own or control most or all property and distribute it out as government experts, scientists, politicians, or occasionally voters see fit. Under socialism, the State puts itself in the place of God and says, "The earth is the State's, and all it contains, the world, and those who dwell in it." … In this view, the State determines our rights, and gives us our freedoms; here there is no appeal beyond the State… Socialism places man, and ultimately the State, in the place of God. Man becomes owned by other men instead of by his Maker. Socialism is an entirely humanistic, God-denying, God-usurping belief… Between these two beliefs–private property and socialism–there exists fundamental conflict. They represent contradictory views of sovereignty, man, law, society, and inheritance.[5]

So, there you have it. Socialism is a belief. And it is a belief very different to Christian belief. Whereas the Christian believes in freedom, freedom of speech, private property etc., the Socialist hands over his/her freedom to the State. Do you think this is overstating

---

[5] Joel McDurmon, *God versus Socialism: A Biblical Critique of the New Social Gospel*, (American Vision Press, Powder Springs, Georgia, 2009).

things? What could go wrong when you entrust your God-given freedoms to the government?

Meanwhile in Scotland…

Religious Hate or Police State?

Rev David Robertson is a Reformed Scottish minister, blogger and podcaster. Says David in a blog,

> Going home the other day I noticed a poster that said: "Dear Bigots, you can't spread your religious hate here. End of sermon. Yours, Scotland." This is part of a series which is also addressed to transphobes, homophobes, racists etc. The only problem is that this is produced by the Scottish Government and Police Scotland.
>
> You state that "A hate incident is any incident that is not a criminal offence, but something which is perceived by the victim or any other person to be motivated by hate or prejudice." By your own criteria your posters, especially the one on religion is a hate incident. I perceive it as being motivated by hate and prejudice.
>
> Why? In my day-to-day life I experience a great deal of anti-Christian prejudice, fuelled by ignorance and prejudice. Your poster will just add to that. You imply that it is religious people who are responsible for what you call homophobia and transphobia (although you don't define what you mean by these terms – is being opposed to SSM 'homophobia'?   Is believing that a woman is a 'female adult

human' transphobia? By not defining your terms you have of course left room for people to claim your support for anything that they determine is 'phobic').[6]

It's like something straight out of George Orwell's Nineteen Eighty-Four! Let's give it a name: Government-creep, or better, Socialist-creep? Political Correctness is another name for Multiculturalism. With this said, the people of Scotland are being told by its social-democratic government that they must conform to the inflammatory rhetoric cited above.

Notice how anti-religious a statement the following statement really is:

"Dear Bigots, you can't spread your religious hate here. End of sermon. Yours, Scotland."

Notice three words that jump out at us: *Bigots*, *religious*, and *sermon*.

Let's start by defining the word "bigot": "A person who is intolerant towards those holding different opinions." English Oxford Living Dictionary. The Collins Dictionary gives a British and an American definition: "A person who is intolerant of any ideas than his or her own, esp on religion, politics, or race." (British). "A person who holds blindly and intolerantly to a particular creed, opinion, etc. A narrow-minded, prejudiced person. (American).

Notice that it is not just "hate" but "religious hate" that is being objected to by the Scottish

---

[6] David Robertson, *Police Scotland and the Scottish Government Reported for Hate Incident*, reported by David to both Police Scotland and the Scottish Government.

Government and Police Scotland. That word "religious", as in "religious hate" is certainly aimed at those who are religious. So is the word "sermon".

What constitutes "religious hate"? We are not told. Is it some Protestant versus Catholic thing? Is it sectarianism, as exampled by some opposing supporters of the Glasgow Rangers and Glasgow Celtic football teams? Again, it is not explained. It is left dangerously undefined.

So, what we have then, is the Scottish Government, in the sentence above, using extreme and evocative language in its short "sermon" with the intent of stirring up a reaction by those who consider themselves to be non-religious towards its religious populace simply for being religious. Result? Instead of simply using the word hate on its own, i.e., by adding the qualifier "religious", the Scottish government is inciting hatred! And without defining what it means by "religious hate" the Scottish Government is the one being bigoted, anti-religious!

Meanwhile back in America…

Saving the West from Socialism

America, that great (Christian) experiment, seems to be getting back on track again. This pleases me. For one who has worked as a marine plumber, domestic plumber, and a railway pipefitter it is good to see American workers of all skin shades getting their jobs back. It's good to see the closed factories reopen. Car plants, steel plants etc. It's like spring has sprung and the winter trees are starting to sprout the green shoots of prosperity, leaves that are for the healing of the nations.

America is the hope of the West, Western Civilization. If America goes under, the West goes down with it. It's that simple! For who will defend the rest of the West against the enemies of our Western democracies?

For all Western democracies there're enemies without and there're enemies within. The enemies without are those Socialist/Communist nations, such as North Korea, China, and Russia. These, and those nations like them, keep an iron grip around the throat of each one of its citizens. When we talk about Western freedoms, we mean the opposite of government micro-management of its people as evidenced by the aforementioned example nations. The enemies within are those who subvert our Western freedoms by applying Socialist/Communist ideologies in the form of excessive government control, from red tape for businesses to thought control through Political Correctness. (I'll use the following "square peg" analogy a fair bit throughout this book just because it is a humorous and apt description) – like a square peg and a round hole, Socialism does not fit into Western Civilization – unless you pound it with a hammer! Yea, even a hammer and a sickle!

What can the West do when it is being beaten over the head with the Progressives' agenda? What can those do whose voice is being drowned out by the irrational Leftist yells of Bigot! Racist! Homophobe! Misogynist! Sexist! Islamophobe! What can the West do in the face of the onslaught of the Political Correctness Brigade? What can those do who wish to dialogue with those they oppose rather than shout them down? Well, they could roll over and admit defeat.

They could drink the Postmodernist Kool Aid. Yes, that's it, just drink the potion and you will feel better, and you will see that Socialism is the best way. Why kick against the goads? Submit!

True confession: I used to be a Socialist, a Marxist Socialist.

A long time ago Vladimir Lenin said, "The goal of Socialism is Communism." However, many years have passed since he said that. Is the Socialism that is now in your face in America really the way to go?

My old college professor wrote a book that could choke a blue whale! It's called "COMMUNIST ESCHATOLOGY: A Christian Philosophical Analysis of the Post-Capitalistic Views of Marx, Engels and Lenin" by Francis Nigel Lee. The point I make is that if anyone knows a great deal about Communism, it's Dr Lee. On occasion he said that Communism does not disappear. He likened the Communist hammer as one pounding on an anvil, swinging back and forth, but with ever increasing intensity. Therefore, Berlin walls may come tumbling down, but don't count your blessings before they're dispatched! Says Eric D. Butler, "[I]n Communist dialectics, retreat is an essential part of the Communist advance!"[7]

I heard Herman Cain on Fox News articulate what we are all wondering when he said, "Socialism has never worked in the history of mankind." In fact, Socialism, like a Winnipeg winter, leaves the fruit-bearing trees of honest industry leafless and bare.

---

[7] Eric. D. Butler, *"Dialectics" Communist Instrument for World Conquest*, Melbourne, (no date) 2.

Indeed, it quietens the voice of the workers through depletion and unemployment. "Workers of the world unite!" Need to feed your family? Just sign on to receive your food stamps!

I have been in the ranks of the unemployed. Loss of job can mean a loss of dignity. A loss of identity. However, when America booms, both dignity and identity are restored to it and the rest of the West. How so? Because that's what Capitalism (as opposed to Communism) does. It means that the individual (rather than the collective) is back in control. It means that "We the People" (rather than the government) are in the driving seat. It means that we don't vote for those who will give us the most handouts because we "feel" that we are entitled to free stuff, but rather we vote for those who will give us the most hand-ups because we "think" that we can contribute to free-dom, our freedom.

Freedom produces prosperity. Socialism? "The toll of Socialism in the last hundred years is 100 million people killed." Dr. Sabastian Gorka on Fox News.

Think about it: No individual Socialist can ever say, "I am free!" How so? "Seemples!" By definition, Socialists are always beholden to those whom they want to be governed by. Whereas Western democracies believe in (lawful) freedom for the individual, Socialism is all about the collective, the mob!

I've lived long enough to see the paradigm shift from thinking to feeling. People used to ask others, "What do you think about such and such?" Now it's "How do you feel about these things?" We've shifted from informed reasoning expressed under emotional control, to emotionalism under the Progressives of whatever political party.

Political Correctness is Socialism by another name. Political Correctness is Social Engineering by Leftists. It is the enemy of the West because it is the enemy of freedom, which freedom includes the basis for every Western democracy, the freedom of speech, i.e., the freedom to speak out in protest against oppressive governments without fear of being locked up or worse, put to death. Whereas, the soap box and the ballot box are how the West expresses this freedom, Socialism through Political Correctness and downright lies seeks to silence those who oppose it.

In her typically humorous way, syndicated columnist Anne Coulter, says the following about the Democrat Party,

> To understand Liberals, one must understand the French Revolution.
> It is difficult to track the precise chronology of the French revolution because there is no logic to it, as there never is with a mob. Basically, the mob would hear a rumor, get ginned up, and then run out and start beheading people. Imagine CodePink with pikes. From beginning to end, the French Revolution was a textbook case of the behavior of mobs…
> Liberals don't like to talk about the French revolution because it is the history of them. They lyingly portray the American Revolution as if it too were a revolution of the mob, but merely to list the signposts of each reveals their

different character. The American Revolution had the Minutemen, the ride of Paul Revere, the Continental Congress, the Declaration of Independence, and the Liberty Bell.

The markers of the French Revolution were the Great Fear, the storming of the Bastille, the food riots, the march on Versailles, the Day of the Daggers, the de-Christianization campaign, the storming of Tuileries, the September Massacres, the beheading of Louis XVI, the beheading of Marie Antoinette, the Reign of Terror, and then the guillotining of one revolutionary after another, until finally the mob's leader, Robespierre, got the "national razor." That's not including random insurrections, lynchings, and assassinations that occurred throughout the four year period known as the "French Revolution."[8]

"When the enemy shall come in like a flood, the Spirit of the LORD shall lift up a standard against him." Isaiah 59:19b (KJV). Enter Donald Trump.

Says Joel McDurmon,

Yes, the Berlin Wall fell, but it fell in our direction. No one talks about this. The Soviet Union fell, but Marxism and Socialism have long flooded all of Western and Eastern Civilization. America is no exception. Marxism is history, yes, and yet the

---

[8] Ann Coulter, *Demonic: How the Liberal Mob is Endangering America*, (Crown Publishing Group, a division of Random House, Inc., New York, 2011), 99-100.

influences of Marxism and various ideas of socialism have never been more dangerous than now, when it stands ready to expand further into every office of government, and when we are yet asleep to it.[9]

I live in Australia where we still, at this point, await our 'Donald Trump'. Those who love Western freedom love the way this man was voted in as President – against just about every poll and in the face of a hostile media that's in the grip of the Progressivist agenda. Indeed, apart from a few outlets, the American media could be called the propaganda wing of the Democrat Party which has, especially since the advent of Bernie Sanders, shifted away from the moderate politics of JFK, to now even openly embracing Socialism and Socialist candidates.

President Trump wishes to, as he calls it, "Drain the swamp", by which he means remove from power "establishment politicians", (i.e., whether Republican or Democrat), those that feather their own nests by kowtowing to the interests of lobby groups rather than the will of "We the People", along with the sinister "Deep State". "The Donald" is so successful financially that he cannot be "bought" by bribes. He is the champion of the people, the worker, looking out for their needs, the needs of America as a whole. He believes in the rule of law, American Law in accordance with its Constitution, and not some European Law written by a group of Socialists!

---

[9] Joel McDurmon, *God versus Socialism: A Biblical Critique of the New Social Gospel*, (American Vision Press, Powder Springs, Georgia, 2009), 26.

President Donald Trump is making America great again, i.e., he is getting America back on track with the "Cultural Mandate" (see e.g., Genesis 1:26-28). If the end (i.e., goal) of Socialism is Communism then the end of Capitalism (i.e., Biblical Capitalism) is the glory of God! Says Donald Geddes,

> Marxist Socialism is intractably opposed to Christianity hence anyone who stands for Christian values is treated with derision… Marxism seeks to replace the sovereignty of God with the sovereignty of man.[10]

Lord, please raise up a standard for Australia just as You have for America. Please save the West from Socialism.

Meanwhile back in Scotland…

Private Property

The idea of private property is not a human invention. It comes from God: "The earth is the LORD's, and all its fulness, the world and those who dwell therein" Psalm 24:1.

Own a piece of property and you are free to develop it and/or things on it. Says William Federer,

> If someone owns land, they can accumulate possessions. The Bible called this being blessed. Karl Marx called this capitalism."[11]

---

[10] Donald Geddes in an article in an email mail-out.

[11] William J. Federer, *Rise of the Tyrant*, Volume 2 of *Change to Chains-the 6,000 Year Quest for Global Power*, (Amerisearch, St Louis, Missouri, 2015), 123.

And there's the rub. I have lived for many years in three different countries in which I have seen that the basis of liberty, i.e., owning private property, has always had to stand vigilant guard against Marxist marauding forces.

I grew up in a social housing estate in a low socioeconomic area of Scotland. To be sure, these were in the decades when Scotland was still recovering from the economic devastation of WWII with its attendant social upheaval. The words of Lonnie Donegan sum it up where he sings, *"Oh, my old man's a dustman/He wears a dustman's hat/He wears cor blimey trousers/And he lives in a council flat."* Your guess is as good as mine as to what 'cor blimey trousers' are, but we all know what a council flat is. For the English it is their castle – "An Englishman's home is his castle."[12] For the Scots it's their "wee bit hill and glen"[13] that their ancestors fought and died for – even if they have noisy neighbours living above them and also through the walls. Thus, the landed gentry in Scotland with their family pile and sprawling estates with their "No Trespassing – Private Property" signs were either at best envied or at worst despised or both by the "huddled masses yearning to breathe free."[14]

---

[12] Term used in a law established by in 1628 when Sir Edward Coke wrote *The Institutes of the Laws of England*, which included the line, "For a man's house is his castle, *et domus sua cuique est tutissimum refugium* [and each man's home is his safest refuge]."

[13] Line from a Scottish folk song written by Roy Williamson of the folk group *The Corries*, and presented in 1967.

[14] A line from "The New Colossus", a sonnet that American poet Emma Lazarus (1849–1887) wrote in 1883. In 1903, the poem

Sometimes a few drinks would help some Scots "breathe free" with the idea of liberty. Will Fyffe illustrates this in the lines of his song, "I Belong To Glasgow" where he sang, "I'm only a common old working chap as anyone here can see/But when I get a couple of drinks on a Saturday, Glasgow belongs to me." We need more than a couple of drinks to gain our freedom as individuals. For, as Lord Acton says, "Property, not conscience, is the basis of liberty."[15]

I had left Scotland and had settled in Canada by the time the much despised by the Scottish Left, Margaret Thatcher took control of the Scots. In the 1980s Miners' Strikes were the order of the day when I returned to Scotland for a visit. However, I did see glimmers of liberty arising in the form of new front doors adorning council flats. I asked a friend, "Whit's wi' the fancy new front doors on yer coonsil hooses?" I was told that it was Thatcher. She was letting people purchase the council houses they had been paying rent on for years. Freedom! As a symbol of that newfound freedom the ex-council house domicile would install a new front door of their own choice. Dignity, human dignity was slowly being restored. Says Lesley Riddoch,

> Scots tended to live in council-owned, not private, property. In the 1970s Scotland built

---

was inscribed onto a plaque and mounted on the base of the Statue of Liberty.

[15] Lord Acton.

proportionally more public sector homes than Eastern Europe.[16]

Noah Webster of *Webster's Dictionary* fame wrote, "Let the people have property and they will have power." Conversely, the removal of the people's power comes from the State owning all the property and renting out bits of it to its huddled masses. And on and on it goes as Capitalism, with its sword and shield of freedom, has to defend itself against the invading forces of Socialism and cut off the thieving heads of the Government Leviathan.

We speak in general terms, but, allow a man or a woman ownership of a plot of land and you allow them ownership of dignity. Let's, for a moment, return to Lord Acton: "Property, not conscience, is the basis of liberty." I can have the liberty of a clear conscience even while behind bars as a man falsely accused. But true liberty comes through the ownership of private property. Therefore, the shackles of State slavery are removed by ownership of private property for the individual citizen.

One of Glasgow's weans, Gerry Rafferty, (now departed), in his 1970s song "Baker Street," (which is a sad song with a hint of hope towards its end), anyway, there're the lines which say, "He's got this dream about buying some land/He's gonna give up the booze and the one night stands/And then he'll settle down/In some quiet little town/And forget about everything." "Buying some land" is Biblical.

---

[16] Lesley Riddoch, *Blossom: What Scotland Needs To Flourish*, (Luath Press, Edinburgh, 2013).

Therefore, private property is a good thing. Never despise the things of God.

William J. Federer says,

> Ancient Israel was the first nation with private land ownership – the promised 'LAND.' … Numbers 26:52-56: And the LORD spake unto Moses, saying, Unto these the land shall be divided for an inheritance according to the number of names. To many thou shalt give the more inheritance, and to few thou shalt give the less inheritance: to every one shall his inheritance be given according to those that were numbered of him. Notwithstanding the land shall be divided by lot: according to the names of the tribes of their fathers they shall inherit. According to the lot shall the possession thereof be divided between many and few. Deuteronomy 27:17: Cursed be he that removeth his neighbour's landmark.[17]

"Landmark", in case you don't know, is a boundary stone, a border marker. In other words, don't steal any of your neighbour's private property, and that goes for governments, even Socialist governments, too. "Thou shalt not steal" Exodus 20:15 – "By these words the right of property received formal acknowledgment, and a protest was made by

---

[17] William J. Federer, *Rise of the Tyrant*, Volume 2 of *Change to Chains-the 6,000 Year Quest for Global Power*, (Amerisearch, St Louis, Missouri, 2015), 121.

anticipation against the maxim of modern socialists –
'La propriete, c'est le vol.'"[18]

Meanwhile back in Scotland, Canada and
Australia…

Politics & Religion

As in Scotland and Canada, so in Australia: a
general rule of thumb is that politics and religion
should be avoided in general conversation lest an
argument ensue! What is a minister (whether political
or religious) supposed to do? These are two of my
favourite subjects! In the Christian-influenced West,
while politics focuses mainly on State affairs, religion
focuses mainly on Church affairs. Some refer to this as
the "separation of Church and State" by which term is
meant that Church and State are sovereign spheres and
operate as such in each respective nation.

Church and State are but two aspects of any one
nation, i.e., one nation under God. These apply both
tables of God's Moral Law, but each in their respective
sphere. The first four of the Ten Commandments focus
on love for God and the last six deal with love for
neighbour. Thus, the summary of God's Law is: Love
God and your neighbour as yourself. (*cf.* Matthew
22:36-40). Says Rousas John Rushdoony,

> [W]e do not equate government with the state.
> To do so is totalitarianism. Government is first
> of all the self-government of man; it is also the
> family, the church, the school, our vocation,
> society and its institutions, and finally, civil

---

[18] Pulpit Commentary.

government. Our problem today is that government is equated with the state, an anti-Christian view.[19]

The nation that works best is one in which the Church and State are kept distinct but not separate. A nation is a family. It is also a political and a religious entity. It is one as the Triune God is one and it is many as God, the Triune God, is many. As Father, Son, and Holy Spirit are distinct (but not separate), so the spheres of Family, Church, and State are distinct (but not separate). As in the Trinity, each sphere compliments and penetrates the others.

There are aspects of God's Law that specifically apply to each of these three spheres, e.g., in the sphere of the Family it can be seen that the 5th Commandment, *Honour thy father and thy mother*, and the 7th, *Thou shalt not commit adultery*, have special application. In the sphere of the Church, e.g., the 2nd, *Thou shalt not make unto thee any graven image*, the 3rd, *Thou shalt not take the name of the LORD thy God in vain*, and the 4th, *Remember the Sabbath day, to keep it holy*, have particular application. And in the sphere of the State, e.g., the 6th, *Thou shalt not kill*, the 8th, *Thou shalt not steal*, and the 9th, *Thou shalt not bear false witness against thy neighbour*, have direct application. However, if a nation is to remain united

---

[19] Response to Ed Dobson and Ed Hindson, "Apocalypse Now?: What Fundamentalists Believe About the End of the World," *Policy Review* (Fall 1986), 6, 17-22. Rushdoony's response appears in the Winter 1987 issue of *Policy Review*. Quoted by Joel McDurmon, The biblical origins of separation of Church and State.

(i.e., one, just as God is one), then it would do well in each sphere to encourage the keeping of the 1st, *Thou shalt have no other gods before me*, and the 10th, *Thou shalt not covet.*

To be sure, no one is saved (i.e., justified in the sight of God) by their own keeping of God's Moral Law. Jesus Christ is our only Saviour. However, about nations Scripture says, "The wicked shall be turned into hell, and all the nations that forget God" Psalm 9:17; "Righteousness exalts a nation, but sin is a reproach to any people" Proverbs 14:34. It is the role of the State to reward good (righteousness) and punish evil (sin/crime). Whereas the Church holds keys, the State bears the sword. The former opens and closes Heaven to the nation's citizens by the proclamation of the Gospel and the latter rewards good and punishes evil by upholding and enforcing the law.

Consider the 4th Commandment as an example of where the Commandments overlap both Church and State at a national level. The State could and should ensure that its citizens are given opportunity to have quality family time, as well as time to gather as the Church to worship God, simply by applying and enforcing Sunday as the national day of rest. Of course, essential services would need to remain open, fire, police, ambulance, hospitals, not to mention the cows needing to be milked and the chickens fed etc. Duties of necessity and mercy still need to be performed. The Bible is clear on this.

The 10th Commandment clearly demonstrates the need for the distinction between Church and State under God. The mere thought of the State trying to enforce this Commandment conjures up images of "thought police" as illustrated by the present "Political Correctness" movement's stifling "free speech". This happens when a State forgets or rejects its Christian, i.e., Biblical mandate.

The Reformation, to lesser and greater extents, set the law-abiding citizens of Western nations free from interference from Church and State. Citizens of nations that turn their back on God's Law and Gospel are destined to return to the type of bondage the pre-Reformation people experienced. Hence this book!

A nation has many aspects, three of which are Family, Church, and State.

The Church has many aspects, three of which are the governing bodies of the board of elders (or local church Session), Presbytery, and Assembly.

The State has many aspects, three of which are local government, state government, federal government.

The more these spheres, Family, Church, and State, work in harmony with God's Law as their basis, and their basis of unity, the greater the freedom for that nation's citizens. For then everyone learns and knows the difference between good and evil, because each sphere is operating from the same manual. And when everyone knows the difference between good and evil, then the Church can do its job more effectively, pointing sinners to the only Saviour of sinners, Jesus Christ. By far the most obedient citizens in any God-honouring nation are those that have been reconciled to God in Christ.

If we are to honour God at a national as well as an individual level we will need to think nationally and talk more about politics and religion, not less! As Jesus says, "Go therefore and make disciples of all the *nations*, baptising *them* in the name of the Father and the Son and the Holy Spirit, teaching *them* to observe all things that I have commanded you" Matthew 28:19-20.

Whoever came up with the idea that we should never bring up politics or religion in conversation is a genius, an evil genius! Let's see, we're not supposed to talk about what the best way is for people to live together as God has revealed it to us in His Word. Why? Because it may cause division? In other words, we've just shut up about these things! But I put it to you, it is precisely because of this ludicrous idea that there is so much tension, yes, even among some Christians.

I did a random online search for the words religion and politics. Here's a typical generic definition for both:

> Religion: The belief in and worship of a god or gods, or any such system of belief and worship. Politics: The activities of the government, members of law-making organizations or people who try to influence the way a country is governed.

Let's see if I've got this. I'll try to summarize those definitions of religion and politics in one brief sentence: As a Christian, I'm not to discuss how the Triune God of the Bible wants me to influence the way my country is governed! Why not? Oh, its because it may interfere and even hinder the way that the evil genius who invented the daft idea that religion and politics ought to be avoided in conversation. This is anti-Christian! Yet, tragically, even some Christians apparently believe this kind of tosh.

As you may or may not know, Christians are magnificent at complicating the simple. Staying on our subject of religion and politics, let's consider a couple of lines from the "Great Commission."

Jesus says to His Church, "Therefore go and make disciples of all nations, baptizing them in the name of the Father and of the Son and of the Holy Spirit, and teaching them to obey everything I have commanded you. And surely I am with you always, to the very end of the age" (Matt. 28:19-20 NIV. I used the NIV because that seems to be the most popular version used today).

Talk about making the simple complicated? That word "baptizing" has caused endless disputes among Christians over its meaning and its related mode. However, let's focus on the words "disciples" and "nations" seeing as this relates directly to those two *verboten* subjects, religion and politics, i.e., the belief in the God of Scripture and how He wants countries governed.

First, *disciples*. Is this word simply referring to the word nations in the Great Commission or the more complicated idea of people who comprise these nations? Is it about making all nations disciples, just as Jesus had done with the nation of Israel back then? Or does Jesus mean that His Church is also to make the rest of the nations into what He had made the nation of Israel, i.e., a discipled nation, (you know, the olive tree that already is Israel and now the simple idea is that the other nations are to be discipled too, i.e., ingrafted into the same tree? Or is this too complicated?)

Second, *nations*. Like the Hebrew nation, the ethnics, the Ethnoi, i.e., the non-"Jewish" nations, are to become part of the same entity, as the Gospel goes forth from Jerusalem also into the various nations of the world to leaven the whole batch of dough as it were.

Bottom line? We'll let that great Bible commentator Matthew Henry (1662-1714) help us to keep it simple. We'll let him sum it up for us. (Please look up Matthew Henry's Commentary online for the full version of the following on Matthew 28):

> The commission which our Lord Jesus received himself from the Father. Being about to *authorize* his apostles, if any ask by what authority he doeth it, and who gave him that authority, here he tells us, *All power is given unto me in heaven and in earth;* a very great word, and which none but he could say. Hereby he asserts his <u>universal dominion</u> as Mediator, which is the great foundation of the Christian <u>religion</u>. He has *all power*...
> How far his commission is extended; to *all nations*. Go, and disciple *all nations*. Not that they must go all together into every place, but by consent disperse themselves in such manner

as might best *diffuse* the light of the gospel. Now this plainly signifies it to be the will of Christ, *First,* That the covenant of peculiarity, made with the Jews, should now be cancelled and disannulled. This word broke down the middle wall of partition, which had so long excluded the Gentiles from a visible church-state; and whereas the apostles, when first sent out, were forbidden to go into the way of the Gentiles, now they were sent to *all nations. Secondly,* That salvation by Christ should be offered to all, and none excluded that did not by their unbelief and impenitence exclude themselves. The salvation they were to preach is a *common salvation;* whoever will, let him come, and take the benefit of the *act of indemnity;* for there is no difference of Jew or Greek in Christ Jesus. *Thirdly,* That <u>Christianity should be twisted in with national constitutions</u>, that <u>the kingdoms of the world should become Christ's kingdoms</u>, and <u>their kings the church's nursing-fathers</u>…

What is the principal intention of this commission; to *disciple* <u>all</u> nations. *Matheteusate—"Admit them disciples;* <u>do your utmost to make the nations Christian nations;"</u> not, "Go to the nations, and denounce the judgments of God against them, as Jonah against Nineveh, and as the other Old-Testament prophets" (though they had reason enough to expect it for their wickedness), "but go, and *disciple them*." <u>Christ the Mediator is setting up a kingdom in the world</u>, bring the nations to be his subjects; setting up a school, bring the nations to be his scholars; raising an army for the carrying on of the war against the powers of darkness, <u>enlist the nations of the earth under his banner</u>. The work which the apostles had to do, was, to <u>set up the Christian religion in all places</u>, and it was honourable work; the achievements of the mighty heroes of the world were nothing to it. They conquered the nations for themselves, and made them miserable; <u>the apostles conquered them for Christ, and made them happy</u>.

Matthew Henry, would no doubt be familiar with the Geneva Bible first published in 1560 and with the more up-to-date (at least for him) 1599 translation which spells out what Henry has just elaborated on, "Go therefore, and teach all nations, baptizing them in the Name of the Father, and the Son, and the holy Ghost, teaching them to observe all things, whatsoever I have commanded you: and lo, I am with you alway, until the end of the world, Amen." (Matt. 28:19-20).

So, before the simple became sooooo complicated, the idea was that Christians were commissioned to bring Christ's religion and His politics to all the nations. Notice that Jesus says that we are not doing this on our own or in our own strength, for He says, "Lo, I am with you alway (sic), until the end of the world. Amen." It is Christ who is building His Kingdom. (We'll leave what is meant by the "end of the world" for another time!) This is the simple easy-to-understand meaning of Christ's Great Commission, make all nations disciples of Christ. Now, here's a brief description of some of the complicated versions.

- Why bother with the Great Commission. The whole world is going to burn up anyway!
- What's the use? Everything is going to grow worse. Tribulation!
- Quick, try to make some converts because we are about to be Raptured any day now and the pagans are going to be Left Behind, (as has been said since the early 1800s)!
- Christ has two Kingdoms, one for the pagans and the other for Christians. Don't ever confuse them! The former can rely on Natural Law and the latter God's Law (but only the good bits!)
- Separation of Church and State. Stay in your lane. Alter the Westminster Confession of Faith 1648 (especially Chapter 23, paragraph 3 *Of the Civil Magistrate*), which, with the Westminster Standards, united the four kingdom nations of Scotland, Ireland, England and Wales so that they were one in religion and politics, i.e., a

United Kingdom under the rulership of Christ. We can't have God's justice minsters agreeing with God's gospel ministers now, can we?!

And on and on it goes as the books written defending these positions pile up smothering the simplicity of Christ's Great Commission.

Bottom line? Don't listen to the suggestions of Satan to keep silent about 'religion and politics.' Instead, clear out the clutter and get back to the simple understanding of the Great Commission, the same as the likes of Matthew Henry. "Do your utmost to make the nations Christian nations."

Therefore, sorry dear Christian brothers and sisters but you're going to have to talk to people about religion and politics. Christ has commissioned us to.

Unity in Politics & Religion

The year 2026 is the 250th anniversary of the founding of the American nation. However, after 250 years of theological liberalism and socialism creep we see what happens when Christianity falls asleep at the wheel. It's as Jesus says, "And if the blind lead the blind, both shall fall into the ditch" (Matt. 15:14).

Now the Western nations are under attack from mass migration, Islam, Hinduism, neo-Marxism, Socialism, theological Liberalism, Feminism, Transgenderism, Wokeism, you name it. Why? All because Christians did not "stand fast" on the gospel. If only the West would get back to her Westminster Standards and Three Forms of Unity and be done with all its unbiblical deviations. Let me explain a bit further.

James the VI of Scotland became James I of Great Britain in 1603. He asked for a fresh translation of the Bible. The King James' Version (KJV) was completed in 1611. Though not without much internal friction, at his coronation, James united Scotland, England, Wales and Ireland *politically*, with the intention that God's Word would be the basis of the United Kingdom's social cohesion. Upon James's death in 1625, his son, Charles I, reigned till his execution in 1649. It was during these turbulent times, for the purpose of *religious* and *theological* unity, the English Parliament asked for a Christian Assembly, which comprised of an initial one hundred and forty-two 'learned, godly and judicious Divines,' and thirty-two lay assessors. The *Westminster Standards* were drawn up by the *Westminster Assembly* in 1643–1649. These Standards were to do with Christian teaching and church polity. These formed the basis for uniformity of religion for the United Kingdom of the 1600s, and by extension, the whole of the British Empire from that time forward. In other words, the purpose of the *Westminster Standards* is about uniting Christians, not dividing them.

It was staunch Calvinists like George Whitefield, along with men like the theological professor and signer of *The Declaration*, John Whitherspoon, who proclaimed these teachings during the lead up to the American War of Independence. Witherspoon had a big influence on James Madison and others.

> *John's mother, Anna Walker, could trace her lineage through several pastors back to John Knox himself"*, or that *"In 1746, he led a group of militia volunteers from Beith intent on fighting for King George II against the pro-Catholic Jacobite uprising. Although Witherspoon was not engaged in any military conflict, he was captured and imprisoned for a short time in Doune castle.*[20]

The interesting fact is that Witherspoon, the Scottish Presbyterian who was invited to come over to America to be a professor at what became Princeton, was the only clergyman to sign the American Declaration of Independence – in defiance of King George III. He had a major influence on many of the Founders, no less than one James Madison. The famous converted ex-slave trader, John Newton of Amazing Grace hymn fame, wrote,

> This work has always been regarded as one of the ablest Calvinistic expositions of that doctrine in any language. I hope you approve Mr. Witherspoon's books. I think his *Treatise on Regeneration* is the best I have seen upon this important subject. John Newton (1725-1807) in a letter to Mr. Cunningham.[21]

Even that great slavery abolitionist, William Wilberforce, heaped praise on Witherspoon's theological understanding.

---

[20] Kevin DeYoung, *ibid.*, ix-x.
[21] John Newton, ibid., on dust jacket.

By way of expressing this unity, the very *first* question asked and answered in Westminster Shorter Catechism focuses on the purpose of life. *What is the chief end of man? Man's chief end is to glorify God, and to enjoy Him for ever.* The Larger Catechism expands this a little by replying, *Man's chief and highest end is to glorify God, and fully enjoy Him for ever.*

Christians enjoy God through bringing Him glory. How can we do this? 'So whether you eat or drink or whatever you do, do it all for the glory of God' (1 Cor. 10:31). Like little mirrors reflecting the sun, the purpose of life is to glorify and enjoy God: through food production, culinary skills, agriculture, vinification, beer brewing, whisky distillation, water purification, architecture, education, politics, theology, metallurgy, writing, art, music, preaching and teaching, church attendance, bricklaying, plumbing, carpentry, electrical work, Lord's Day keeping, family, church, state, economics, etc., the list is endless. Yet many Christians reduce glorifying and enjoying God to (occasionally!) attending church for an hour on a Sunday morning.

It was the Gospel of Jesus Christ that made the once great Western nations great. However, nowadays many Christians dualistically compartmentalise the Gospel. The little wheel on a penny-farthing bicycle represents 'God-time' and big one, 'my-time.' If we would only seek to glorify God in everything everywhere, we would surely halt and then reverse the present decline of Western civilisation.

The Christian Gospel is what unites. Socialism is a false religion. It promises a false utopia.

Meanwhile back in Scotland…

A Non-Socialist Looks at Scotland

Scotland is on verge of regaining its independence. I'm in favour of this. Not that I (now living in Australia) have a vote, but, Left-leaning Scots ought not to ostracise non-Socialist Scots (as they are presently doing) if they are to win their independence once again. I suppose my support for an independent Scotland might be classed by some as more heart than head. But I disagree! It's both!

I do try to be Biblical in everything (though I'm not always successful!). It makes perfect Biblical sense for Scotland to be a sovereign nation – even one nation under God (just like America). Indeed, Scotland did have some influence on the founding of "the land of the free and the home of the brave." Says John Eidsmoe,

> Scottish youths who fought for Bonnie Prince Charlie were put to death by the thousands, using the cruellest forms of execution. All forms of Scottish culture, including the playing of bagpipes, the wearing of the kilt, and the speaking of Gaelic, were banned. Hundreds of thousands fled Scotland, most of them finding refuge in North America.
>
> That was in the late 1740s. Thirty years later, in the 1770s, the next generation of Scottish-Americans became leaders in the American War for Independence. In England the war was often called the "Presbyterian Rebellion," and Prime Minister Horace Walpole commented

that "Cousin America has run off with a Presbyterian parson," an obvious reference to Rev. John Witherspoon, Scottish immigrant, President of the College of New Jersey, and a signer of the Declaration of Independence.

In a very real sense, the American War for Independence can be called "Scotland's revenge"… (Footnote 122). In 2014 the people of Scotland voted against independence from Great Britain by a 55%-45% margin, but the Scottish independence movement is far from dead and already there is talk of another referendum.)[22]

Call this war whatever name you may, only call it not an American rebellion; it is nothing more than a Scotch Irish Presbyterian rebellion. – *Anonymous Hessian officer, 1778*[23]

Sure, it wasn't all roses, but God certainly blessed Scotland for its Reformational stance onwards from Knox's "Give me Scotland, or I die!" prayer. Any Scottish tourist-shop's dishtowel "will testify to that"[24]

---

[22] John Eidsmoe, *Historical and Theological Foundations of Law: Volume 2, Classical and Medieval*, (Expanded Second Edition, printed November 2016, Nordskog Publishing Inc., Ventura, California), 787.

[23] Arthur Herman, *How the Scots Invented the Modern World: The true story of how Western Europe's poorest nation created our world & everything in it*, (Broadway Books, New York, 2001), 229.

[24] Reference to a line from the Scottish "The Jeely Piece" song by Adam McNaughton.

– what, with all the lists of inventors with their inventions! Says Arthur Herman,

> The Scots did not invent technology, any more than they invented science – or capitalism or the ideas of progress and liberty. But just as in these other cases, the version of technology we live with most closely resembles the one that Scots such as James Watt organized and perfected. It rests on certain basic principles that the Scottish Enlightenment enshrined: common sense, experience as our best source of knowledge, and arriving at scientific laws by testing general hypotheses through individual experiment and trial and error. Science and technology give civilization its dynamic movement, like the ceaselessly moving pistons of Watt's steam engine. To the Scots, they were the key to modern life, just as they are for us. A rapid succession of Scottish inventors, engineers, doctors, and scientists proved their point to the rest of the world.[25]

Scotland was very industrious. It was a real place of thought and learning. The Enlightenment crowd can put all the spin on it they want, but it was "The preaching of Thy Word and the praising of Thy name" that let Scotland flourish! It was the teaching of the Bible, e.g., that David Hume was wresting with! Adam Smith's Invisible Hand belongs to God! And on

---

[25] Arthur Herman, *Ibid.*, 321-22.

it goes. Arthur Herman points to this unmistakeable Biblical influence where he says,

> At its [i.e., The Scottish Enlightenment's] core was a group of erudite and believing clergymen (unlike the various *abbés* of the French Enlightenment, who were by and large skeptics, and clerics only as a matter of convenience and income). They resolutely believed that a free and open sophisticated culture was compatible with, even predicated on, a solid moral and religious foundation. Robertson and the rest saw the doctrines of Christianity as the very heart of what it meant to be modern.[26]

I am a Capitalist because I believe it is Biblical. Greed? The Calvinist, (including the Scottish Calvinist) is about doing all things to the glory of God. This Protestant or Presbyterian Work Ethic is exemplified by God-blessed endeavours of Calvinists such as, e.g., Arthur Guinness (and Family). A brilliant book that I really enjoyed reading (because it is about two of my favourite subjects) was *The Search for God and Guinness*: A Biography of the Beer That Changed the World, by Stephen Mansfield (2009). Management/employee relations? (Non-government) Welfare? Read this book. It shows the Biblical way how it is done. In fact, (as did I), one ought to throw away one's copy of *The Ragged-Trousered Philanthropist* and swap it for *The Search for God and Guinness*! Says Stephen Mansfield,

---

[26] Ibid., 193.

In the minds of most of the people in the world, Guinness is beer and that is all there is to the story. But this is far from true. Guinness the beer is magnificent, yes, but it is the Guinness culture that for nearly two centuries changed the lives of Guinness workers, transformed poverty in Dublin, and inspired other companies to understand that care for their employees was their most important work. It was the Guinness culture of faith and kindness and generosity that moved men to seek out ways to serve their fellow men, to mend what the harshness of life had torn.[27]

Capitalism, as opposed to Socialism, breeds healthy entrepreneurialism. Says Spike Milligan,

I took my trumpet to war. I thought I'd earn spare cash by playing Fall In, Charge, Retreat, Lights Out, etc. I put a printed card on the Battery Notice Board, showing my scale of charges:
Fall In 1/6
Fall Out 1/-
Charge 1/9
Halt £648
Retreat (Pianissimo). 4/-
Retreat (Fortissimo) 10/-
Lights Out 3/-

---

[27] Stephen Mansfield, *The Search for God and Guinness: A Biography of the Beer That Changed the World*, (2009).

Lights Out played in private … 4/-[28]

Don't let Socialist "spin" put you off (Biblical) Capitalism! The 9th Commandment says, "Thou shalt not lie!" This applies to governments as well as individuals! The role of the government is to provide "a level playing field" for business success. The employees and consumers reap the benefits of business success, higher wages, lower prices etc. The government is not a business, nor is it to operate as a business, for this would be an unfair advantage to legitimate (i.e., Biblical) businesses and would (and does!) result in higher taxes as well as stifling healthy competition among legitimate companies, etc.

Och anyway, I just don't think Socialism can be shown to be Biblical anywhere in the slightest. And, apart from that, empirically, it does not work. Bottom line for me is for less (i.e., limited) government and fewer taxes. The Government is the Referee. Not a Player. It is there to make sure that, from the individual to big business, we all play by the rules (i.e., God's rules). Look, I know that even fellow ministers wonder how we Calvinists derive these teachings from the Bible, but one only has to study The Westminster Confession of Faith, The Shorter and especially the exposition of Ten Commandments in The Larger Catechism – in particular the "Thou Shalt Not Steal" 8th Commandment.

Socialist governments do not have a (Biblical) mandate for their schemes of redistributing (other peoples') wealth! "Thou shalt not steal" applies to

---

[28] Spike Milligan, *Adolf Hitler, My Part in His Downfall,* (Penguin Books, Kindle Edition, 2012).

governments as well as individuals! Infringing the 1st Commandment ("You shall have no other gods before Me") in Socialism, the State becomes god of the people, especially the poor! They become dependent on, (i.e., slaves) of, to, and through the government.

Socialism does not believe in "private property" (i.e., the "Thou shalt not steal" Commandment). This is why Socialistic governments feel "free" to take wealth from one individual or group and give it to another individual or group as it sees fit in accordance with its Socialist or Progressive (read, non-Biblical) agenda.

Socialism and its attendant Social Democracies are a blight on the West and the freedoms we have attained and have enjoyed through the application of Biblical teachings to Western nations and cultures, i.e., Christendom. Thus Socialism is a foreign invader and is the enemy of individual and national freedom.

Scotland: Remember that not all of us are Leftist. Some of us still remember whence we came, where we are, and where we ought to go! Socialism is not the *Scottish* way. It never was. It is not the way because it is not Biblical (apart from the fact that it just does not work!). Sure, many Christians (including Presbyterians!) and many Christian ministers (including "Presbyterian" or Church of Scotland ministers) have been deluded by it. But the Bible gives YOU, (as in you the individual, NOT the government) the mandate to look after the needy. Don't give away your freedom to any government!

Says Rousas John Rushdoony,

The dramatic rise of Marxism coincided with the retreat of Christianity. Marxism offered a saving hope, although a false one, and it parodied the Biblical faith in the sovereign, predestinating power of God with its ideas of materialistic determinism. It has offered victory to a world where too often ostensible Christians have offered instead retreat.[29]

Aye, in Scotland there was and there still is a better way.

Meanwhile back in Social Media…

Who Are the "Mob"?

In America, law abiding citizens had a perfect and legitimate reason to peacefully protest the tragic death of an arrested suspect at the hands of police. Those supposed to maintain and uphold law and order, i.e., the police, by the clearly callous brutality of four policemen caught on video, especially the one who ignored the pleas of a man begging for his life as he, yes, a white policeman, kneeled on a black man's neck, initiated a rapid descent into the chaotic inferno. Then America burned.

Citizens peacefully protested this massive injustice for different reasons. However, all were agreed that, according to the rule of law, George Floyd should not have died in the way he did while in police custody. The policeman who caused his death clearly

---

[29] Rousas John Rushdoony, in Foreword to Francis Nigel Lee's *Communist Eschatology-A Christian Philosophical Analysis of the Post-Capitalistic Views of Marx, Engels and Lenin,* (The Craig Press, Nutley, New Jersey, 1974), vii.

broke the law and is to be tried in accordance with that law. "You shall not murder" Exodus 20:13, i.e., the 6th Commandment.

During the day, some held prayer vigils. Some held placards. Some did both. However, when darkness descended, others rioted. They smashed and burned property, including police cars. And so began Black Lives Matter, the BLM movement. Says Tom Ascol,

> [In] Cultural Marxism ... The working class has been replaced by minorities. Majority groups are defined as 'privileged' and 'oppressive.' Minority groups are defined as 'underprivileged' and 'oppressed.'[30]

The American dream, the "unalienable rights" of "Life, Liberty and the Pursuit of Happiness" was denied to George Floyd and to those hard workers whose businesses literally went up in flames at the hands of the mob. In many cities the police stood idly by and watched the chaos.

My old professor's car bumper sticker proclaimed, "God's Law or Chaos!" Socialism in all its forms is the breaking of God's Law. "You shall not steal" Exodus 20:15, i.e., the 8th Commandment. At its heart, Socialism, as already noted, is about the redistribution of wealth by the government interfering with your lawful pursuit of happiness. Socialism, by this definition, is unlawful, i.e., against God's Law.

---

[30] Tom Ascol in *By What Standard: God's World ... God's Rules*, edited by Jared Longshore, (Founders Press, Cape Coral, Florida, 2020, Third Printing February 2021), 12.

The mob rages against everything America symbolizes, i.e., Life, Liberty, and the Pursuit of Happiness. Not only did the mob burn police cars and local business facilities, it also burned the American flag, the very symbol of law and order. This is anarchy. This is chaos.

The mob hates the Free Market, i.e., what Socialist Karl Marx called "Capitalism". "You shall not steal" applies to the Free Market as much as it does to kids stealing apples. Kids, corporations, and governments all break the 8th Commandment if they steal. Socialism teaches stealing. The mob physically exemplifies this teaching by destroying private property and looting stores. Some of the mob may be what someone has termed "useful idiots"[31], whereby perhaps even unintentionally, some simply go along with the mob's greater goal of collapsing the "Capitalist" system with its attendant rule of law. Revolution is another name for this.

Who or what is behind this ominous subversion? Satan, the "father of lies" immediately springs to mind. He was a murderer and a thief from the beginning. "Fake News" is the breaking of the 9th Commandment, i.e., "You shall not bear false witness against your neighbour" Exodus 20:16. However, Socialism sums up where we are at today. By definition, the mob is Socialist. It is anti-private property. It is anti-America. It is anti-God and anti-Christ. Otherwise it would police itself and maintain law and order

---

[31] "Useful idiots" is a term usually attributed to Vladimir Lenin.

We thank God that all wrongs (including Socialism) have been righted by Jesus Christ. And we look forward to His return.

Stuart McKinlay, my big brother, responded to the above social media post with the following:

> There doesn't seem to be a rush to "like" this excellent item on the nature of a mob, socialism, and a metaphysical explanation for the destruction wreaked in America.
>
> First, your condemnation of the brutal killing of George Floyd is firm: "Those supposed to maintain and uphold law and order, those four policemen, by their clearly callous brutality, especially by one of the policemen who ignored the pleas of a man begging for his life as he kneeled on the man's neck, initiated the rapid descent into the chaotic inferno. Now America burns."
>
> Secondly, though, you go on to denounce socialism, a word cherished in Scotland. It may be that people don't readily equate a rush to the barricades with anything other than an outbreak of outrage that gets out of hand -- rather than (also) a spiritual battle "against God's law".
>
> You explain this in detail, but briefly: "The mob rages against everything America symbolises, i.e., Life, Liberty, and the Pursuit of Happiness... The mob hates the Free Market, what the Socialist Karl Marx called 'Capitalism'.

You equate this with stealing (in violation of the eighth commandment) and thence the path to revolution against capitalism. Yet "socialism" is not understood in these terms in the howfs of the nations, the scene as we know of many powerful intellectual exchanges about anything and everything with many a blow exchanged and nothing much changed as a result.

But socialism is cherished as a fight for justice, a battle against exploitation by rabid employers and rancid landlords, and a defence of the ordinary person from the greed of capitalist predators who have had children down the mines dying for coal while they dine well in refined salons and talk of idlers, sluggards, and the ungrateful poor.

If I may recall a recent conversation, a rickety knowledge of dialectical materialism is, or was, an excellent affectation of we fifth-formers at Vale of Leven Academy in the sixties, as pretentious as Disque Bleu and admiration for the soixante-huitards of the 1968 French student protests, the sixty-eighters.

Vale of Leven was an industrial catchment for a Communism in various degrees of insistence or moribundity: Stuart McKinlay Sen was a sometime adherent, and friends were active - Duncan McGowan, Ross McKenzie, and Willie Lamont from the Renton was the last Communist councillor on Vale of Leven District Council.

That council named the streets of Levenvale after socialists, including (Friedrich) Engels upon whose writings dialectical materialism was drawn as much of those of Karl Marx (ignored by the cooncil). Robert Burns was awarded a street sign too, for being the right sort.

We were all in it together even if we didn't know the thirties Labour leader George Lansbury from George Formby the banjolele player: it was a good thing. Socialism did not seem to be theft, so much as the pursuit of fair pay for a fair day's toil, whoever owns, in Marxist terms, the means of production.

I reckon that many good people, good in the sense that they are considerate of others and function in accordance with a beneficial morality without necessarily any reference to God, though there might be such, are, deep breath, socialists. They could well be sincere Christians or Muslims, or other or none. In fact, they might despise religion as a primitive spiritual diversion from "proper progress" - and still be good people in any reasonable use of the term -- and possibly even be socialists.

I'll leave President Trump to defend himself, but I just thought I'd see if I could encourage the discussion you invite with a very definitive view of socialism…

I responded to Stuart's helpful comments with the following:

"The road to Hell is paved with good intentions" is an old adage that springs to mind regarding your portrayal of those well-intended Socialists. All "good people" are against sending children up chimneys and down mines. But what does any of that have to do with Socialism? What does being rich have to do with Capitalism? Whether rich or poor, an injustice is an injustice because it breaks a just law. Socialism breaks a law, God's Law. Therefore, no matter how well-intentioned any socialist is, he or she is breaking God's Law. And so is any Capitalist who abuses children or their parents.

It's easy to see how Socialism took hold in Scotland in the context of its feudalistic past. Macro feudalism may be aptly illustrated by the micro feudalistic "upstairs downstairs" system in the *taigh mor*, i.e., the "big hoose". The TV series and movie Downton Abbey and the prior *Monarch of the Glen* exemplified this.

America and Australia did not emerge from a feudalistic past. Therefore, it is far easier in these countries to spot an imposter such as Socialism, especially in America with its clearly defined Declaration, Constitution, and Bill of Rights. Unlike America, which is a Constitutional Republic, Australia, like Great Britain is a Constitutional Monarchy, with most of its constitution unwritten or codified.

The paragraph where you say the following gets right to the heart of the issue at hand:

> I reckon that many good people, good in the sense that they are considerate of others and

function in accordance with a beneficial morality without necessarily any reference to God, though there might be such, are, deep breath, socialists. They could well be sincere Christians or Muslims, or other or none. In fact, they might despise religion as a primitive spiritual diversion from 'proper progress' - and still be good people in any reasonable use of the term -- and possibly even be socialists.

Socialism is counterfeit. Hold it up to the light and you will see that any resemblance to Christianity is only coincidental. "Proper progress" comes only with obedience to the God who created us and gave us the manual of how we are to treat Him and each other.

The Bible shows us how to operate in the realm or spheres of Family, Church, and State. Socialism seeks to destroy the family and the church by controlling the state, and thus also destroys the state. Socialism steals from God. It is a thief in the family, (it redefines it), in the church, (it calls it "the opiate of the people" and pretends to be like a "cheerful giver" by its redistribution of other peoples' wealth), and it destroys the state by imposing unbiblical laws on the people, (e.g., unlawfully redefining family, marriage, and humanity, such as infants in the womb).

According to the video footage,[32] George Floyd was unlawfully killed by a law officer. That is the sad irony. Apparently, Floyd was arrested for trying to pass a counterfeit twenty-dollar bill. The

---

[32] Whether George Floyd died from being under the influence of drugs or from being under a policeman's knee or a combination of both, the optics from the video at the time did not look good.

whole thing is tragic travesty of justice and a life was needlessly lost. How did the storeowner know that the $20 bill was counterfeit? How do we know that Socialism is counterfeit? These questions are meant to be rhetorical. However, in case anyone misses it, the answer is the Bible. God's Word addresses things like weights and measures and their misuse and forms of government and their misuses. The trouble is that too many Christians have no idea what the Bible teaches about anything other than how to get saved from going to Hell! (And hopefully, they have a proper understanding of this.)

America was founded on the teaching of the Bible. Its form of government has checks and balances because humans, according to the Bible, are inherently evil. It's separation of powers, judicial, legislative, and executive, are designed to keep each branch honest. The present president, President Trump, [contrary to some accusations!], is doing a good job of acting within his executive jurisdiction. His walk to that church in Washington DC and posing in front of it with God's Word held high in his hand symbolizes what America is, i.e., a nation founded on the rule of law, God's Law.

Stuart, who lives in Scotland, replied to the above with the following:

> The headline news is the last par: "The present president is doing a good job of acting within his executive jurisdiction. His walk to the church in Washington DC and posing in front of it with God's Word held high in his hand symbolizes what America is, i.e., a nation

founded on the rule of law, God's Law." To people looking in: You read it here first.

On socialism: First-class elucidation, and I expected no less. I won't insult you with amateur praise for professional competence and personal sincerity; it is penetrating scholarship offered in easy layman's terms.

I liked particularly, "It's easy to see how Socialism took hold in Scotland in the context of its feudalistic past. Macro feudalism may be aptly illustrated by the micro feudalistic 'upstairs downstairs' system in the taigh mor, i.e. the 'big hoose'."

Once again, I commend it to others to read, too, and of course to discuss it. The space is here.

There was very little of the intended and hoped for interaction with others regarding Socialism on my social media musings.

Says Bobbie Ames:

Socialism as an economic order is a failure. It is retrogressive, not progressive in any positive sense, because it defies God's commandments protecting individuals from the ravages of sinful men. Examples of failures include Medicare, Medicaid, and Obamacare. All stifle free enterprise.

The positions of the socialists against morality include an attack on the nuclear family. For example, they advocate sexual license, abortion, homosexuality, gender fluidity, and the sexualization of children.[33]

President Trump's now famous walk was from the White House to the historical St John's Episcopal Church in Washington DC that had been set on fire by rioters and looters the previous night. He had been accused of hiding, cowering in the basement of the White House. Religious and non-religious Trump haters piled on with their predicted feigned outrage and condemnation of him for doing this, i.e., standing front of a burned out and boarded up church with a Bible in his hand. In reference to this I placed the following tongue-in-cheek post on Facebook:

> "God, I thank you that I am not like other men. I actually enter church buildings. I actually open the Bible. I actually read from it..."

I received a couple or so "likes", but, lest anyone miss my point, I followed it with the Parable of The Pharisee & The Tax Collector, to which my Facebook post alluded:

> Then Jesus told this story to some who had great confidence in their own righteousness and scorned everyone else: "Two men went to the Temple to pray. One was a Pharisee, and the other was a despised tax

---

[33] Bobbie Ames, *Land That I Love: Restoring Our Christian Heritage*, (Nordskog Publishing Inc., Ventura, California, 2020), 195.

collector. The Pharisee stood by himself and prayed this prayer 'I thank you, God, that I am not like other people—cheaters, sinners, adulterers. I'm certainly not like that tax collector! I fast twice a week, and I give you a tenth of my income.'

But the tax collector stood at a distance and dared not even lift his eyes to heaven as he prayed. Instead, he beat his chest in sorrow, saying, 'O God, be merciful to me, for I am a sinner.' I tell you, this sinner, not the Pharisee, returned home justified before God. For those who exalt themselves will be humbled, and those who humble themselves will be exalted. Luke 18:9-14 NLT.

The self-righteous have deemed President Trump to be a cheater, sinner, and adulterer, and thus unfit in their eyes to be president. Whether true or not, whatever his past, President Trump has been good for the "worker", for business, and for the so called Black and Hispanic "communities". He has been good for America.

Meanwhile back in Western Civilisation…

Western Politics

Voting in Australia is compulsory. Therefore, unlike Scotland where the citizens are *free* to reject the candidates in an election simply by staying at home, rain, hail or snow (or weather in which you could fry an egg on the sidewalk), Australians have to drag themselves to the polling booth in order to 'spoil' the ballot if they wish to reject all the candidates! Yes, some are not happy with politics and others would substitute 'politicians' for 'Cretans' in the adage "Cretans are always liars" Titus 1:12.

Why would politics cause some to speak so? It might be a whole range of issues including economics, taxes, national roads, abortion, marriage redefinition, refugees and a whole lot more. We try to vote-in politicians who share our views on these and such-like issues. Therefore, Western political systems depend on the honesty of their political candidates.

Some would claim that an honest politician is an oxymoron. But is this a fair assessment of Western politicians and politics? Well, it doesn't help the cause of politicians when we see them never directly answer any questions when being interviewed. No doubt they ramble on about their "talking points" out of fear of the "gotcha" questions whereby some interviewers purposely set out to trip them up in their speech. Thus, the derogatory term "spin doctor" has been used of certain politicians.

Should Christians give politics a wide berth? I know of at least one Atheist who thinks Christians ought not to become politicians because they cannot separate their religion from their politics! One can only wonder at the arrogance of this sort of anti-Christian and therefore bigoted view of Christians and politics in light of the fact that there is still a Christian majority in most Western nations. However, and more to the point, it is thanks to Christianity that we have democracy in the West in the first place! If it is true, (and it certainly is) that the West was built on the back of Christianity, then that which is contrary to it would be sand in the gearbox.

Lenin, Marx, and Engels introduced Atheism into Western politics with their different flavours of Socialism in which the citizens ultimately serve the State rather than God, by which the God-given rights of the individual began to give way to the imposed will of the collective. (Some Christians blindly and foolishly still buy into various shades of Socialism!)

Then came the "thought police" in the forms of the KGB and SS etc., in the 20th century. These have morphed into the Political Correctness (PC) movement of the 21st where it is now difficult even to discuss issues without being demonized for disagreeing with the narrative of "mob thinking". Says Joseph Boot,

> Far from dead, the Marxism of the new left is manifest as ecological and spiritualised socialism that seeks an androgynous, classless, discrimination – and distinction-free world of 'social justice' – a world ruled by a scientific, socialist, pagan elite.[34]

The West was built on the Westminster-system of politics which in turn was built upon Biblical principles. Presbyterianism still clearly displays those biblical principles. There is an "issue" (or a motion). There are those who speak for the motion and there are those who speak against the motion. There is a moderator (or referee). After the issue has been discussed sufficiently by both sides, it is then put to a

---

[34] Joseph Boot, *The Mission of God: A Manifesto of Hope for Society*, (Wilberforce Publications, London, 2016), 164.

vote. The majority wins. This is Western democracy in practice. It is Christianity in politics. Of course, it is adversarial, but no one is shouted down and drowned out by *ad hominem* attacks. This is freedom of speech.

Because of this system we tend to have a two-party system, i.e., those with left wing views of the issues and those on the right. Yes, some politicians are Independents, but they too tend to be either left or right on most issues. Always remember, "The first *one* to plead his cause *seems* right, until his neighbour comes and examines him" Proverbs 18:17.

Political Duopolies

Grocery shopping can be a boring but necessary chore. You gotta eat! So off you go to to buy some bread and milk, but instead you end up strolling up and down the aisles hoping for an occasional bargain. You are unaware of the 'elevator music' playing in the background to help make your 'shopping experience' as relaxing as possible. The products at eye level are the most popular because, em, they're at eye level. Items on sale are simply subsidised by a cyclical raising and lowering the prices on other items.

In Australia we have two major grocery stores, Woolworths and Coles. Sure, there're other supermarkets, such as Aldi and IGA. However, these, like Ma and Pa corner grocery stores, don't have the regular selection of items sold in Coles and Woolies.

Like Coles and Woolies, we have another duopoly in Australia, the Labor Party and Coalition Party. We are being forced to (yeah, fined if we don't!) vote for either party in the political duopoly. Sure, like the supermarkets, with Aldi, IGA, et al, there're independents and candidates from minor parties. However, when we visited the polling booth on Saturday 3rd May 2025, it was to be involved in the election of one member of the duopoly.

Some prefer Coles for their meat products and other prefer Woolworths for their vegies, (or is it the other way round?). Anyway, both are essentially selling the same stuff. Indeed, we refer to the Liberal/National Coalition Party as 'Labor-lite'. Net-Zero (the issue of climate change) being the main sale item that the duopoly is trying to sell us. This is the eye level elephant in the room that fewer voters are buying. Should we buy our green lightbulbs from Labor or Labor-lite?

I watched one of the debates between the two candidates from the duopoly: Dull and Duller! A trip to the supermarket would've been more exciting!

When I vote in Australian General Elections, I look for a local candidate who I think best lines up with what the Scriptures have to say about governments and government leaders, i.e., God's ministers to us for good (Rom. 13:4). Do any of these candidates even read the Bible? Do they know what is good and what is evil so that they can promote the former and deter the latter? Do they even know that they are God's ministers? Do they favour Marx over Jesus? Are they more into wealth redistribution (Socialism) than small government and fewer taxes (Christianity)? Do they know that God's 8th Commandment applies to governments as much as individuals? "You shall not steal" (Exod. 20:15).

I recommend that they pipe-in some soothing elevator music to help the voter relax as we walk down the aisle to cast our votes at the checkout, sorry, voting booth.

Yes, we all know that whoever we vote for will have a direct effect on how much we pay at the grocery checkout; power bills; petrol; rates; taxes and all the rest.

Meanwhile back in America…

Christian Freedom or Socialist Bondage?
The Americans had to suffer eight long years of the Obama presidency. So did the rest of the West! During which President Obama managed to polarize Americans like never before. Everything on the Obama side of politics is seen in terms of race, gender, or whichever "tribe" you identify with. Hence, "Identity Politics" whereby people are hired because of the colour of their skin, and now it's not just race, but add to that sexuality, gender, perceived gender etc, instead of merit. This is most divisive for any nation. Says Voddie Baucham,

> Cultural Marxism ... reduces everything to race, class, and sex. Cultural Marxism divides people up slightly differently than Classical Marxism. Classical Marxism divides people up into the bourgeoisie and proletariat, the haves and the have nots - between those who control the means of production and those who do not. In Cultural Marxism, you divide the world

between those who establish and benefit from the cultural hegemony and everyone else. Those who do not benefit from the cultural hegemony are oppressed by it. For one reason or other, they are not part of the dominant group. Ethnic Gnosticism is rooted in this Cultural Marxist paradigm.[35]

Arguably, President Obama and his regime clandestinely concocted and had passed "Obamacare" (i.e., socialised medicine) behind closed doors and furtively foisted it on an unwilling majority of Americans. Of course, this is not exactly how President Obama would describe this turn of events in America. And that's the point. He never seemed to be able to see, let alone acknowledge, the damage he was doing to the very fabric of the (Christian) Republic of America. For, at least twenty of the fifty states were seeking to sue the Federal Government on and around the (un)constitutionality of the Federal Government's *forcing* individual Americans to buy one of its products on pain of a fine. We never heard anyone say about the health-care system, "If it ain't broke don't fix it." Everyone knew it needed to be improved. But Obamacare went way, way too far. Says The Epoch Times,

> U.S. District Judge Reed O'Connor in Fort Worth, Texas agreed with a coalition of 20 states that a 2017 change in tax law to eliminate

---

[35] Voddie Baucham in *By What Standard: God's World ... God's Rules*, edited by Jared Longshore, (Founders Press, Cape Coral, Florida, 2020, Third Printing February 2021), 106.

a penalty for not having health insurance invalidates the entire Affordable Care Act, also known as Obamacare law. O'Connor's decision is likely to be appealed to the U.S. Supreme Court.[36]

All these Affordable Care Act (ObamaCare) disputations can cause the head to spin and the brain to hurt. Is ObamaCare really socialized medicine? A big bit or a little bit? How do we define socialized medicine? Regardless, if you know anything about today's Democrats and their lurch further to the left, then it's not hard to predict the ultimate goal of Obamacare. Here's a quote from one person who perhaps, to use a Biblical phrase, sees the writing on the wall. Says Robert Tracinski,

> Forcing insurers to cover people who are already sick and to charge them the same rates as healthy people has jacked up insurance premiums for everyone else. So because the law didn't make insurance affordable, Congress has to make it affordable by heavily subsidizing it with even more of the taxpayers' money… From the very beginning, I have argued that ObamaCare was ultimately designed to fail. Its basic contradiction is that it was founded on a fundamental hostility toward the entire idea of health insurance, which Obama and the Democrats view as inherently parasitical. Yet the Affordable Care Act is a scheme to require mandatory, universal

---

[36] *The Epoch Times*, (by Reuters), December 14, 2018.

purchase of the very product they despise. How do you square that circle? Simple. ObamaCare mandated and subsidized the purchase of health insurance, but on terms that obviously made it unfeasible over the long term. Obama did so on the presumption that Democrats would be able to come back later and blame the fiasco on those greedy private insurers, then go for what they really wanted all along: a "public option" modeled on Medicare, as a further stepping stone toward "single payer," i.e., socialized medicine.[37]

Socialism is the *forced* redistribution of wealth. This, therefore, is not Christianity in any way, shape, or form. In opposition to this, the Bible teaches "Thou shalt not steal", (this goes for governments as well as individuals), and charity for the Christian is a voluntary thing (e.g., the Lord loves a "cheerful" giver), not a forced thing. When it comes to cheerful giving, some have been known to go above and beyond. Says Spike Milligan humorously,

> For three years I had been trumpet player with the Ritz Revels, a bunch of spotty musicians held together with hair oil. They paid ten shillings a gig; of this I gave Mother nine, who in turn gave seven to the church for the Poor of

---

[37] Robert Tracinski, *Obama: ObamaCare Didn't Work, So Let's Completely Socialize Medicine*, (The Federalist, July 15, 2016).

the Parish. I couldn't understand it, we were the Poor of the Parish.[38]

Is paying your fair share of taxes Biblical? Maybe yes and maybe no. (Depends what you mean by "fair".) However, Obamacare is not about loving one's neighbour as oneself. Rather, it is about the government harassing one and one's neighbours to pay another's (medical) bills! This is socialism, and it is nothing like what the Christian founders of America had in mind when they wrote the Constitution and Bill of Rights etc.

Speaking of the American Bill of Rights, Salvatore Babones says something interesting,

> What a lot of people don't understand about the American Bill of Rights is that it is not really a Bill of Rights. It's a list of freedoms. It's a list of things that Americans told the government you can't interfere with this. As an American I don't have a right to free speech enforced by a government board. I have the simple freedom of speech and the government is not allowed to regulate that right.[39]

Christianity is about (collective and individual) freedom under God, even at a national level. Socialism is simply bondage by and to the State because the U.S. Federal Government was in the process of forcing its

---

[38] Spike Milligan, *Adolf Hitler, My Part in His Downfall,* (Penguin Books, Kindle Edition, 2012).
[39] Salvatore Babones, *The Outsiders*, Sky News, 13 December 2018.

people to involve themselves in its socialised medicine plan (on pain of government retribution). This caused people to wonder if President Obama really is some kind of socialist. Says Joel McDurmon,

> Nowhere does the Bible authorize civil rulers to distribute or redistribute wealth or resources. The Bible distinctly specifies which crimes the civil government has the power to punish.[40]

If any were brave enough to criticize President Obama and any of his policies, they were immediately shown the "racist card." One only has to remember what the leftist media said about Sarah Palin and all Conservative Americans back then, (e.g., the "Tea-Partiers"). They were demonised by the leftist (i.e., the mainstream) media. This only served to polarize America further.

It is no longer about politics in America, whether a person is a Republican or a Democrat. Rather the lines are being drawn on whether one is a Constitutional American or a Socialist American.

America is THE great Christian experiment. As a Christian I am greatly encouraged to see Americans at a grass roots level seeking to regain their Christian heritage, their freedom under God, as they (re)discover their (Christian) Constitution. Whether at a federal, state, or individual level, may America live up to her constant boast before the world: "In God we trust."

---

[40] Joel McDurmon, *God versus Socialism: A Biblical Critique of the New Social Gospel*, (American Vision Press, Powder Springs, Georgia, 2009), 104.

Christian freedom or Socialist bondage? We watch and pray. For if America falls to socialism, what hope, at this time, have the rest of the nations?

Meanwhile back in Scotland...

"Should Scotland be an Independent Country?"

"Should Scotland be an independent country?" Not so long ago the people of Scotland were asked to answer this question in a national referendum. What do *you* think? Well, here is what I think. I think that this is a redundant question. I think that this question is merely rhetorical! I think that this question is simply a device being used to awaken the residents of Scotland. I think that there is a lot of wisdom behind this question!

How so? Well, because we now see that the tide is turning on the polls in favour of independence as the question works its way into the hearts and minds of the people. The question has certainly been working its way under people's peely-wally and freckled skin! However, the question is wise in that it is far from establishing any sort of racial superiority of Scots. For, the credentials needed to vote in this referendum are proof of current residence in the geographical region of Scotland. Therefore, ethnicity is a non-issue. However, as a non-resident I am always excluded from casting a vote either way.

Perhaps the downside is that as one who was foreign born but raised in Scotland I, like many others of a similar situation, feel (i.e., think!) as if I should have a say in this referendum. Why? Well, I have been an unofficial ambassador for Scotland and all things Scottish for over a decade throughout Canada and now over three decades in Australia. I have promoted the food and drink of Scottish culture, her dance and music, her native languages, i.e., Gaelic and Lallans. I have spoken highly of her geographical location and her topography. I have promoted the bonnie banks of Loch Lomond and her attendant Ben Lomond, not to mention Loch Ness and her "monster!" I have written stories about Scotland and have written and sung many songs about Scotland in clubs and at various events over the long years. Alas! all this and more did not qualify me to vote in the referendum of 18 September 2014.

Should the current residents of the geographical region of what used to be Scotland continue to vote against becoming a country again then I and those like me will never be able to become Scottish. I know that this must sound strange to those residents who were waging the NO! campaign. I am sure this is because they had not yet fully thought through the issue as a whole. I say this because I had seen countless video clips in which those who are campaigning against Scotland becoming a country again say things like, "I love Scotland. I was born here. I am Scottish and I am British!" By saying that you are British you might as well also include that you are European and that you are an Earthling! What's wrong with just being Scottish?

I have no reason to believe that these people were not trying to be truthful, but they were clearly not in tune with what was going on! <u>The whole point of the referendum was about the current residents of Scotland becoming Scottish!</u> Clearly many on the NO! side are missing this. However, though it is too late for that Referendum, it is never too late for the penny to drop. In for a penny, in for a pound, (Sterling that is).

As any passport holder will attest, presently the residents of the geographical location that used to be Scotland (i.e., the place pre-1707) are now British not Scottish. Says Lesley Riddoch,

> Still, who can blame English folk for using British interchangeably? In population terms, eight times out of ten, they are right… Thirty-four million Canadians are regularly called American and 4.4 million Kiwis are confused every day with Australians. But nations that are also states can shrug it off. After all, they can reinflate squashed national identity with usefully tangible symbols: passports, flags and national anthems. Scotland cannot.[41]

One cannot simply become Scottish until the residents of the geographical location known as Scotland answer in the affirmative the question that was put to them on 18 September: "Should Scotland be an independent country?"

This question answers itself. To ask it presupposes that Scotland is not presently a country! Scotland will remain as a non-country until and unless her current residents democratically vote that it should once again be a country. Until they vote in favour of independence, and the resultant changes based on independence, are subsequently affected, the residents of the geographical location that used to be Scotland

---

[41] Lesley Riddoch, Blossom: *What Scotland Needs To Flourish*, (Luath Press, Edinburgh, 2013).

will remain British (regardless of their food and clothing, music and languages, highlands and islands, hills, lochs and lowlands). Independence means that you become like Canada, Australia, America, New Zealand, Jamaica, *ad nauseam.*

Like President Trump, the Scottish National Party is Nationalist! The Party always has been. And over the many years I have never heard anyone suggest that being a Nationalist was anything other than being a Patriot, i.e., putting your own nation's wellbeing first before any Globalist agenda. And, like President Trump, the Scottish National Party has to contend with false propaganda in the form of "Fake News". Regarding the BBC's role in Scotland's referendum on Independence, says GA Ponsonby,

> Like most of Scotland's media, its IN Scotland but not OF Scotland. It does not reflect the views of Scotland but instead lectures Scotland. The BBC is an institution that cannot change in order to meet the needs of Scots, but one that tries to force Scots to adapt to the needs of the British state. This is why BBC Scotland manipulates news. It isn't informing the Scottish public, it is trying to influence us.[42]

Here, one is reminded of President Trump combating the false propaganda constantly put out by the Washington DC establishment (i.e., both Republican and Democrat). As did the BBC during the Scottish Referendum, the establishment, by using a

---

[42] GA Ponsonby, *London Calling: How the BBC Stole the Referendum*, (NNS Media Ltd., 2015).

Trump-hating wing of the media, works overtime in its attempt to maintain its influence over the American people through mis-reporting, negative spin and downright lies. Trump, by use of Twitter, is able to by-pass the biased filter of the status quo establishment and directly inform his voter base, i.e., the American people. Do you want to know what President Trump actually said? Then read his tweets! Straight from the horse's mouth, as they say. This is President Trump's effective method of "draining the swamp", as he calls it, i.e., through exposing incompetent and/or corrupt politicians and their attendant media spin. But I digress (again).

I do not have the vote, but Scotland I have breathed your air. I have eaten your food. I have drunk your water (and still drink your whisky!) I have studied both of your native languages. I have played the side drum in your pipe bands. I have studied your bagpipes. I have walked on your hills and I have swum in your lochs. I have rowed on your rivers and your lochs. I have listened to the patter and chatter of your peaty burns. As a wean I have climbed your trees. I have sledged down your snow-clad hills. I have been pricked by your thorns and your thistles. I have scars on my fingers, knees and elbows from falling off bikes and bogies going down your braes. As an adult I have drank in your pubs. I have eaten in your restaurants. I have been educated in your schools. I have worked in your industries. I have married one of your daughters. I have studied your history. I have read poetry and stories, and theological treatises from your best writers. I have studied your philosophy and your theology. I have read about your long list of inventors.

I have seen your vast and positive contributions to the (now) independent countries of Canada and Australia.

Residents of Scotland realise your greatness! Realise what you have and who you are! Why O why did you not then condescend long enough on 18 September 2014 to put your mark on the ballot paper where it says "YES!" in answer to the wise and rhetorical question: "Should Scotland be an independent country?" It is almost an insult to common sense to be asked this! Next time, for the sake of freedom, just do it!

Meanwhile back to the Bible…

Gospel Freedom

Arguably the Westernized nations are testimony to the success of the Gospel of Jesus Christ. To cut the long story short, the freedoms we enjoy in the West came about after the Christianisation of these nations. (An oversimplification, yes, but nevertheless true!) To be sure, some Western nations were/still are more Christianised than others, but clearly the leaven of Christianity, i.e., the Biblical teaching of God's Law and Gospel, has permeated the West. This is to say that God's Ten Commandments along with the right spirit for keeping them are the foundations upon which Western societies are built. Loving God and others as yourself, doing unto others as you would have them do unto you, is the application of God's Law in the West.

However, God's Ten Commandments for a lawful society are now being shunned by some in favour of a plethora of rules and regulations belonging to Secular Humanism – a movement which is trying very hard to assert itself in the West. E.g., in America they've been dragging out all reference to God's Ten Commandments from its Law Courts, universities and schools etc. In place of God's Law, as a cat drags a dead animal into the house, so the Trojan Horse of Secular Humanism has been dragged into many American Institutions. Multitudes of blood-sucking, life draining maggots of death are pouring forth from this over-flogged dead horse!

In the West we are losing our Gospel Freedoms to big government red tape. The West is now very much entangled in the sticky web of Political Correctness. The spider of thought-control continues injecting its venom into and numbing the minds of the many peoples. Marxism is the new opiate of the masses! Says Joel McDurmon,

> Even though his system was consciously atheistic, Marx's humanism took the place of religious law by default.[43]

Now people cannot be trusted to do the right thing, i.e., no Gospel Freedoms. Now, we are being treated like little kids again: No Running, No Smoking, No Swearing, No Foods, No Drinks, No Tee-shirts, No This, No That, No the Next Thing! No, No, No. No… Rules, rules, and yet more rules! Oh, the burden is too great to bear! Like a fly in a spider's web, we are being more and more entangled in the sticky RED tape of Political Correctness! Bring back the TEN (10)

---

[43] Joel McDurmon, *God versus Socialism: A Biblical Critique of the New Social Gospel*, (American Vision Press, Powder Springs, Georgia, 2009), 33.

Commandments and please get rid of all your millions of rules!

Neo-Darwinists, such as the outspoken Richard Dawkins, have the freedom to say what they like about Christians and the Triune God. Muslims also get to blaspheme Christ and the Triune God also with impunity. Yet, as soon as Christians say anything about Neo-Darwinism we are ridiculed, expelled from science class, and made to sit in detention with the loony fringe! Any Muslim who hears the Good News of Jesus Christ, and repents and believes it, becomes the target of death threats, if not death itself at the hands of a group of people who allege that Islam is a religion of peace! Says Ann Coulter,

> Russia has a good education system, probably better than ours – but then, so does Burkina Faso. Putin is fighting ISIS and refuses to accept the Muslim "migrants" swarming through Western Europe.
> The number one enemy of Western civilization today isn't Russia. It's Islam.[44]

Bring back the Gospel Freedoms that we in the West used to enjoy before those people started using their freedoms as licence to de-Christianise the West.

Islam sees the endorsement, encouragement and promotion of the homosexual lifestyle, pornography, prostitution, etc. as Christianity's failure in the West. However, in many ways, when you really

---

[44] Ann Coulter, *Resistance is Futile! How the Trump-Hating Left Lost its Collective Mind*, (Sentinel, New York, New York, 2018), 214.

think about it, these things, although debauched in themselves, are evidence of the Gospel's success! The West simply has to learn that with Gospel Freedom there also comes Gospel Responsibility. Just because we have the freedom to do a thing doesn't make that thing the right and good thing to do.

God's Ten Commandments and all their applications in Family, Church, and State keep us on the right track. So let's get back to the Gospel Freedoms we once had. Otherwise *Shariah* Law (i.e., Islamic law) will be the order of the day for the West (i.e., for those who haven't lost their heads!)

Meanwhile back to Trump…

Trump 2.0

The Gospel sets us free. And we must stand firm in that freedom. "Stand fast therefore in the liberty by which Christ has made us free, and do not be entangled again with a yoke of bondage' (Galatians 5:1).

At its founding, the USA got the Gospel right, and God blessed America. To be sure, the founders ought to have mentioned Jesus in their 1776 Declaration of Independence and their 1789 Constitution. But the "Life, Liberty, and the Pursuit of Happiness" line stirs complacent and even recalcitrant hearts to take notice.

Could you imagine what it would be like to leave a country where there is no freedom of speech? We take all the freedom we have for granted. Well, some countries shoot people for complaining about government policy. It must have been great being a refugee from one of these countries, sailing into New

York for instance. There's the Statue of Liberty up ahead. You're on a boat full of people fleeing the bondage of persecution. Then someone on the boat tells you about this great statue you see growing taller as you grow closer. They quote to you some of the words written on it:

> Give me your tired, your poor,
> Your huddled masses yearning to breathe free,
> The wretched refuse of your teeming shore.
> Send these, the homeless, tempest-tost to me,
> I lift my lamp beside the golden door!

Alas! America opened her borders to the world from 2021-2025. Along with those "yearning to breathe free" came sex and child-traffickers, thieves, rapists, murderers, who robbed, raped, pillaged and murdered their way across the USA. Obviously, these were not exercising the freedom that comes from the Gospel but were clearly illustrating by their actions that they were still in bondage to sin. There was an unforgettable scene at the end of the first *Planet of the Apes* movie. Charleton Heston (who played Moses in *The Ten Commandments*) is walking along a sandy beach. He sees the neck and shoulders of a great object jutting out of the sand. It's the Statue of Liberty half-submerged. Enter Donald J. Trump.

Trump "lost" the 2020 election which took place during the fog and smog of the COVID-19 pandemic. We all went to bed with Trump well in the lead while the vote-counting continued, only to rise in the morning to hear about truckloads of postal votes that had swayed the election against him. Mollie

Hemingway wrote a book about this weird event titled, *RIGGED How the Media, Big Tech, and the Democrats Seized Our Elections*. With eighty-four pages of endnotes, she accurately details how the 2020 US election was rigged. She writes, "This book rose out of a desire to do what the media failed to do: investigate how the election was handled in a year when states, counties, and cities rapidly changed their election procedures with minimal oversight."[45] Hemingway also wrote,

> The 2020 election is just the tip of the iceberg. The left's vehement anti-Trumpism – and willingness to lie, contort reality, and ruin Trump's supporters to advance its agenda – has undermined half the country's faith in America's most vaunted institutions. Restoring that trust will take a gargantuan effort. And regrettably, it does not look like anyone in the political and cultural establishment is willing to do the work required to do so.[46]

Then followed the four years of open borders, multiple fake Trump impeachment trials, from lunatic "Russian Collusion" nonsense to fake rape accusations. Trump spent months attending a New York court defending his good name. This was "lawfare" on steroids! Despite the very pits of hell being arrayed against him, the voters voted in the "too

---

[45] Mollie Hemingway, *RIGGED How the Media, Big Tech, and the Democrats Seized Our Elections*, (Regnery, Washington DC, 2021), 333.
[46] Ibid., 330.

big to rig" 2024 election. The 45th president became 47th.

Trump switched from *Twitter* to his own *Truth Social* social media outlet. Twitter was bought over by Elon Musk and shifted from being a Leftist propaganda platform to being more of a "free speech" platform. Having learned from his first term as president, this time round, because he could clearly see during the interim four years all those who were the furtive players, from dodgy army generals to backstabbing politicians, Trump was able to drain "the swamp" even more. Because of their ungodly and demonic smear campaigns, the Democrats were confident that Trump had no chance of ever winning again. They thought their trumped-up charges applied by activist judges would ensure that the bad "orange man" would be wearing an orange jumpsuit in some prison. But alas! the forces of neo-Marxism were slowed down if not halted in the USA – for now.

The Democrat Party has been taken hostage by the extreme left of its party. It is no longer the party of JFK. Now it is all about same-sex marriage, transgenderism, and locking up anyone who disagrees with abortion, even late term abortion, state education policies, open borders, illegal immigration, etc. In other words, it demonises and shouts down and tries to shut up and even lock up any who disagree with its politics.

Even here in Australia I have personally witnessed what has become known as Trump Derangement Syndrome (TDS). This phrase was initially coined by the late Charles Krauthammer (1950-2018) to refer to vitriolic responses and reactions to George W Bush when he was president. Regarding President Trump, I have witnessed people go into "meltdown" at the mere mention of Trump's name! They have become something resembling a toxic bubbling and smouldering heap of sulphuric acid such as may happen when a car battery is dropped on concrete.

Not the most reliable go-to source for accurate information, *Wikipedia* says that "Trump Derangement Syndrome (TDS) is a pejorative term used to describe negative reactions to U.S. president Donald Trump that are characterized as irrational and disconnected from Trump's actual policy positions." Another word for TDS is pure hatred of a man, which, as Wikipedia surprisingly accurately states, is "irrational and disconnected." Someone needs to write a doctoral dissertation on TDS. TDS is sin! And, as my old theological professor would say, "Often we cannot figure out sin, because sin is irrational."

Why does the mention of President Trump create such a negative reaction in some people even here in Australia? A lot of this can be traced back and attributed to Saul Alinski's *Rules for Radicals'* approach of demonising your political opponents, as mentioned earlier, by calling them names – Racist, fascist, misogynist, Islamophobe, homophobe, transphobe, bigot etc., etc. Thus, like acid being thrown in a person's face, or turning a blowtorch on him/her, your opponent is inundated and blasted with vitriolic hate and hatred. Make no mistake, to demonize your opponent is to spread hate. We now can see the success of using this method for extending the Socialist's cause. Exhibit A: TDS.

One is reminded of Saul who, after his conversion to Christianity, became the Apostle Paul. Speaking of before his conversion, when he used to persecute the Church, we are given a picture of Saul's heart where it says, "Saul, [was] still breathing threats of murder…" (Acts 9:1a). Now, it is argued by some, that because Donald Trump has not understood that the way of salvation is through faith, not of works (Eph. 2:8-9), he cannot possibly be a Christian. That being understood, Scripture says, "Whoever hates his brother is a murderer, and you know that no murderer has eternal life abiding in him" (1 John 3:15). The general principle here is that, just as a man lusting after a woman who is not his wife has committed adultery with her in his heart has broken God's 7th Commandment (Matt. 5:28; Exod. 20:14), so hating someone in your heart is breaking the 6th Commandment (Exod. 20:13; Matt. 5:21-22; Rom. 13:9). Disagreeing with someone's politics is one thing, but fuelling hatred is another.

Socialism is a worldview. In other words, Socialism is a religion. Some Christians have been fooled into thinking that Socialism is a form of Christianity endorsed by the Bible. Nothing could be further from the truth! Neo-Marxism is its most militant form of expression. Though Socialism poses as a movement about loving your neighbour, like Islam, it has been exposed as a religion of hate. Trump 2.0 has been used by God to warn Christians to shun it.

Trump & The Trinity

In some ways the USA is like a great train engine. The Western nations, indeed, the world's nations, are like the carriages the American motive power pulls. That engine had been sidetracked, nay, it had been derailed for four years with the Biden presidency. However, with the re-election of Donald J Trump, the engine is back on track and now the carriages are beginning to pull in behind.

God has been kind. Wokeism has been defeated by the ballot box. We can now talk freely once again. We can agree to disagree with the Left and their Political Correctness without them shouting us down with all their Saul Alinsky demonising tactics. They may continue to call us racist, Islamophobic, misogynistic, homophobic, transphobic names, but, because they have been sprung, their Neo-Marxist catcalling now falls on deaf ears. The world has awakened to them and their destructive strategies. The rebuilding has begun.

Revival is no longer the domain of the giant marquees along the sawdust trails in America. It is now in the universities and halls of government. The Leftist Bishop of the Washington DC Episcopalian Church, by lecturing President Trump and the rest of the congregation on the very things that had just decisively been defeated in the election, showed to the whole world that Wokeism was as much in the Church and in the State. Now the cleanup begins. Gospel expansion continues. The doors and tent flaps of the Revival marquees have been removed. "Enlarge the place of your tent, and let them stretch out the curtains of your dwellings; do not spare; lengthen your cords, and strengthen your stakes. For you shall expand to the right and to the left, and your descendants will inherit the nations, and make the desolate cities inhabited" (Isa. 54:2-3).

The Serpent's head was crushed by the Seed of the woman at Calvary. The war against evil has been won by Christ and the weapon of His cross. America and the West had forgotten this. The purveyors of Wokeism are like those jungle fighters of WWII that didn't know the war was over. Peace has broken out once again. The Prince of Peace has won the day. Lay down your arms and bow the knee to the Saviour of sinners, swear allegiance to Him and go and sin no more.

Trump and the Trinity means that he and the Republican Party, at the federal level, have won back the State. The State is not the Nation but is only one important aspect thereof.

The following is excerpted from a book which I coauthored with D Rudi Schwartz called *The Kingdom: Every Square Inch.* If there are two main Bible teachings that many Christians don't seem to know much about, they are Politics and the Trinity. Many Christians detach Politics from Christianity and, along with this, they also detach Western culture and civilization from the Trinity. The error here is in the misunderstanding and misapplication of the separation of Church and State, which in turn was left wide-open to became the Leftist mantra of the separation of God and State. See where Trump and the Trinity come in in the following:

Christians ought to seek to advance the Kingdom of Christ only in accordance with God's design (Gen. 1:26-28; 9:9:1-7; Exod. 20:1-17; Rom. 13:1-7). When it comes to nations, State Constitutions must be shaped by natural law, but need to be illuminated by the light of Scripture, especially the Ten Commandments and their 'general equity' applications as exemplified throughout the whole of God's Word.

'Sphere sovereignty' or, as it is sometimes known by its apt description, 'differentiated responsibility', is a reflection of the Trinity seen in creation in the light of Scripture. Thus, the Scriptures must be studied if we are to arrive at a proper understanding of what a nation is, and how God would have that nation function.

If the doctrine of the *ontological* Trinity were expressed in human terms as a nation, then Family, Church, and State would interact and interpenetrate each other while each would remain sovereign in its own sphere of function. In other words, as are members of the Family, so are members of the Church and members of the State; all are members of the one nation. Like each Person in the Trinity being distinct from the Others yet all are one, it is the same for the three main pillars of the nation…

Redemption has to do with what Christ has redeemed, as in purchased, bought back. To leave the State operating according to natural law in terms of common grace, when Christ has commissioned Christians to teach the nations to obey His law, is to be disobedient, even cruel. For example, State-sanctioned abortion on demand is infanticide. What Christian in their right mind would approve of this? It boggles the mind to think that there are Christians who believe that Christ has left places in nations where Satan and those he has blinded can hide. No! Every square inch belongs to the King.

The State owns the sword of justice and, as such, is Christ's minister for justice. It exists to promote good and punish evil, therefore, it is a *religious* entity. It reflects aspects of Adam's role in the garden, i.e., "*to cultivate and to keep it.*" In this way the State exemplifies the biblical concept that culture is religion externalised. Even though it wields the instrument of death, the State is to cultivate life in its nation. Thus, why the State needs also the light of Scripture. The punishment must fit the crime and not go beyond it. An "eye for eye" means *equitable* compensation for the victim, and not a life for an eye (Exod. 21:24; Lev. 24:17-22; see also where Jesus corrects the greedy abuse of the law of compensation, Mat. 5:38-42).

The Church owns the sword of the Spirit, yes, with the keys of the Kingdom. Just as a screwdriver or other such implement can be used to prise the lid off a paint can, so the sword of the Spirit can and must be used to lift the lid off the State's suppression of the truth (Rom. 1:18) so that even the State is without excuse for ignoring God. "*For his invisible attributes, namely, his eternal power and divine nature, have been clearly perceived, ever since the creation of the world, in the things that have been made. So they are without excuse*" (Rom. 1:20 ESV)…

It needs to be noted, a) that hints of the ontological Trinity can be seen in natural law, glimpses of the Creator and Redeemer God which the unredeemed suppress in unrighteousness, and b) because Two Kingdom Theology eschews sphere sovereignty, wherever this aberrant form of (R2K) theology is to the fore, sooner or later the State will be seen pushing its foot in the door of the family home, and eventually marching in and trampling underfoot the God-given rights of Family. The Church, likewise, will be persecuted by unlawful State intrusion. The implementation of sphere sovereignty (by the Spirit with His Word changing hearts) will guard against this. Thus, and therefore, to advance the Kingdom, we are to take Christ's gospel and law to the nations as per the King's Great Commission. R2K stands for Radical Two Kingdoms. This Two Kingdom Theology unnecessarily divides Christ's Kingdom on earth.

> Creating a dichotomy between a sacred kingdom and a common kingdom, as Two Kingdom Theology postulates, assumes that the common kingdom is ruled by natural law and the spiritual kingdom by the moral law. There exists a single kingdom—Christ's Kingdom—which fulfils the promises of God as outlined in the covenant of grace. Within this kingdom, various spheres of authority and

guidance operate, all subordinate to the Kingship of Christ.[47]

The function of the State is to serve and protect the nation, i.e., its people and its borders. The State is its guardian. To withhold the fruits of Christ's redemption from the State is akin to suppressing the real reason for its existence, and it puts that nation in jeopardy of God's covenantal judgment upon disobedience. Like the Family and the Church, in any nation, the State exists to glorify God. We hear echoes of God's covenant promise to Abraham in Genesis 12:3 in the following, *"For the nation and kingdom which will not serve you shall perish, and those nations shall be utterly ruined"* (Isa. 60:12; Zech. 14:17; Rev. 21:24). Here is one of those places that unites those purveyors of dualism such as Dispensationalism with its nation destroying separation of the people of Old Testament Israel with the New Testament Church, and Two Kingdom Theology with its sacred and secular division between Church and State. For the Dispensationalist, the Church is that spiritual entity that is going to be 'raptured' off the planet earth so that the Lord can once again get back to working with His so called 'chosen people' in the modern-day nation of Israel – as if the Church is not made up of His chosen people, both Jew

---

[47] Neil Cullan McKinlay & D. Rudi Schwartz, *God's Kingdom: What! On Earth?*, (Weemac Publishing, QLD, Australia, 2026), 79. See also by the same authors, *The Kingdom: Every Square Inch*, 119.

and Gentile! (Gal. 3:26-29). Yes, Christians *are* Abraham's offspring.

Dispensationalism has a faulty view of the Church, and Two Kingdom Theology has a faulty view of the State. However, they are united in their over spiritualising of the Church to the point that the blessings of God given to Abraham and his seed remain hidden from the nations, hidden behind the Church's four walls. Here we see the difference between Church and Kingdom. Christ has *one* people, His Church. And He has *one* Kingdom, the good news and blessings of which are to be spread to every nation by the Church. Family, Church, and State are the three main pillars that support every nation. Get between or remove any one of these three pillars (through Rapture Theology or Two Kingdom Theology) and that nation is in grave danger of perishing. Two Kingdom Theology weakens the pillar of the State by withholding from it the spectacles of Scripture.

When we study the Mona Lisa, our eyes are always drawn to the centre of her face, her nose, with the intriguing smile underneath and above are those hypnotic eyes that follow you around the room. Natural grace, as it were, leaves you wondering if Da Vinci designed things that way. Particular grace, so to speak, explains the Fibonacci Sequence to you and how Da Vinci used this mathematical wonder of God's creation, the "Golden Ratio". From nautilus shells to violins to music to oil paintings, God receives His glory only when His designs in creation are utilised and He is acknowledged for them.

God has designed the State, in its own sphere of function and operation, to serve and protect the nation and every lawful sphere thereof that operates therein. To the glory of the Triune God.

Meanwhile back in Ireland (and Australia)…

Ireland (and Australia) Redefine Marriage

The Republic of Ireland voted in favour of changing its constitution in order to permit same-sex or homosexual marriage. The people have spoken! Democracy lives in Ireland! However, is the redefining of marriage a wise thing?

Apparently 4% of the Irish population identify themselves as either homosexual/lesbian or bisexual. Sure, the figure may be more due to some wishing not to disclose their sexual preferences, but the figure certainly includes homosexuals who are against redefining marriage.

Be that as it may, what was wrong with the definition that marriage is between one man and one woman forever (i.e., till death) that the Irish now wish to change it? Well, apparently the Irish wish to bring in "marriage equality," suggesting that somehow marriage has been unequal up till now. The idea is that if two men or two women "love" each other then these same-sex couples ought to have the "right" to be allowed to enter into holy matrimony.

The Irish voted to give them the right by changing the very definition of marriage. Australia followed suit and changed marriage from meaning "the union of a man and a woman to the exclusion of all others, voluntarily entered into for life", now to mean that marriage is "the union of two people to the exclusion of all others, voluntarily entered into for life". Apparently, this gives same-sex couples the "right" to get married. But what about the rights of any children that might become included in these unions? Says Margaret Somerville,

> Same-sex marriage … forces us to choose between giving priority to children's rights or to homosexual adults' claims.[48]

Not that I'm a regular domino player or a gambler, but by choosing homosexual adults' rights over children's rights has to cause some sort of domino effect, which in turn will affect each of the three basic and fundamental institutions of any Westernised nation, i.e., the Family, the Church, and the State. Western civilisation acknowledges, or used to acknowledge, that these three institutions were instituted by God, and are/were sacrosanct.

Think about it, over the centuries wars had been fought, much blood had been spilt, and great treasures had been spent, all in order to bring the West to its present success and greatness. Think of the Reformation, the Founding of America, the Scientific and Industrial Revolutions, the Enlightenment and all the great freedoms we gained from doing away with Papal and Sovereign rulership. No longer does the Church rule over the State and the Family or the State over Church and Family or the Family over Church

---

[48] Professor Margaret Somerville AM. The Australian, July 23, 2011. (Quoted in *Stealing from a Child: The Injustice of 'Marriage Equality'*, Connor Court Publishing Party Ltd, 2016 by David Van Gend.

and State. Western democracies put "We the People" back in control. Family, Church, and State, each lawfully governing in its own sphere of sovereignty without unlawful interference from the other institutions. However, by redefining marriage, the State is now interfering in the Family and the Church. It can only ever end in a pile of fallen dominoes!

The Roman Catholic Church (which is big but waning in Ireland) considers marriage to be one of its seven sacraments. Therefore, this new definition of marriage cannot be incorporated into its Church dogma without papal authority. If we remember that this is a church that, for example, without Biblical authority tells its priests that they cannot marry, then we will understand that perhaps it may very soon be swayed by public opinion. However, for Biblical Christians the issue is simple. The question is: Is same-sex marriage Biblical? In other words, does God's Word teach that marriage is only between one man and one woman forever? Of course it does! And there is the rub. Jesus in Matthew 19:3-6 by referring us to Adam and Eve in Genesis 1 and 2 is clearly teaching us that marriage ought only be between only a mature male and a mature female.

Regarding the whole movement that seeks to redefine everything that helped to make the West great, including marriage, in Australia, Conservative *News* said that Conservative Party spokesman Lyle Shelton said,

> "Now that so many politicians have uncritically embraced the rainbow political movement, they need to be honest with

Australians about where the gender agenda ends and what it means for children and for public policy. We were told there would be no consequences to de-gendering marriage but all we have seen over the past 12 months [i.e., since redefining marriage] is increased pressure to jettison the biological understanding of gender in schools, on birth certificates or in women's sport."
Mr Shelton said people struggling with their gender should of course be respected and treated with dignity but that did not mean gender should be redefined for the rest of the population.[49]

To be sure those who do not care what the Bible says about marriage do not care if two people of the same sex get hitched. Some people may be indifferent to this issue. However, the majority of those who voted in Ireland have, as have the majority of those who voted in Australia, consciously and unequivocally voted to endorse and promote homosexuality in their society. Is this a good thing? What does the Bible say?

I don't recommend that anyone call God any names as usually happens when anyone attempts even to discuss any of society's current issues, but the Bible takes a very scientific or empirical approach and calls all homosexual acts "unnatural." So that you do not miss what the Bible teaches about homosexual acts consider the following: Someone once used the "square peg" analogy in the following manner, "A square peg in a round hole may be possible with a bit

---

[49] Conservatives.org.au

of force – but it is ugly!" Homosexual "marriage" endorses sodomy and buggery and other unnatural acts. And for the record God also forbids such unnatural actions between a male husband and his female wife. For He says in His Word, "Marriage should be honoured by all, and the marriage bed kept pure, for God will judge the adulterer and all the sexually immoral." Hebrews 13:4 (NIV).

Ordinally, marriages usually produce offspring, i.e., the marriage turns into a family. Says Tucker Carlson,

> Supporting marriage and children is the best, maybe the only way, for Republicans or any of us to save the country [i.e., America].[50]

Says Australian author David Van Gend,

> The evidence shows that the institution of homosexual "marriage" would bring various forms of harm to the children of such unions. Which of our politicians is so negligent, so captive to fashion, so indifferent to the best interests of the child, as to sign such an institution into law?[51]

Some may conclude that what two consenting adults (two males or two females) do in private is their business but the whole of the voting public of Ireland

---

[50] Tucker Carlson on Tucker Carlson tonight, Fox News, 8 November 2018.
[51] David Van Gend, *Stealing from a Child: The Injustice of 'Marriage Equality'*, (Connor Court Publishing Party Ltd, 2016).

(and Australia) have made it their own personal business. The majority has voted to redefine marriage to include what the Bible describes as something unnatural (see e.g., Romans 1). That is Ireland's (and Australia's) prerogative as a sovereign state. But is it wise? The Bible says it isn't. However, the people of Ireland (and Australia) have spoken. About Australia, David Van Gend says.

> [O]nly 1.2% of the Australian population identify as homosexual, while 97.4% identify as heterosexual.[52]

And what about abortion? There were celebrations in the streets on 25 May 2018 and following in Ireland when the Irish voters decided 68 to 32 percent to overturn their Eighth Amendment and legalise the killing of their babies! I watched news footage of people in tears of happiness and rejoicing over the future death of infants. Bizarre! Extremely bizarre!

Meanwhile back to the Bible…

Healthy Pulpit Healthy Nation
"O wad some Pow'r the giftie gie us
To see oursels as others see us!"

---

[52] David Van Gend, *Stealing from a Child: The Injustice of 'Marriage Equality'*, Connor Court Publishing Party Ltd, 2016, citing Anthony, Sex in Australia, Sexual identity, sexual attraction and sexual experience among a representative sample of adults, *Australia and New Zealand Journal of Public Health 27, no 2 (2003): 138-145.*

We agree with the Scottish poet Robert Burns: Seeing ourselves as others see us "wad frae mony a blunder free us." But let's say that some Power gave us the gift to see a whole nation as others see it. Wouldn't that be something? Well, when the Almighty opens someone's eyes he or she is able to see the nation, even the whole world, as Christians see it. We now enter into the world of worldviews.

Ted Baehr, the founder and Publisher of Movieguide, helps us to understand what we mean by the word "worldview" in the context of socialism. Says Ted,

> A worldview is a way of interpreting reality. Although political ideologies are not technically worldviews, they often display attributes or qualities similar to worldviews. For example, the communist writer Karl Marx said that his communism was the ultimate humanism and advocated that humanist society should abolish religion, family, nation, and private property. That is one reason why Movieguide has a separate worldview content category for communism. Movieguide also shows readers when a movie merely has a moral or biblical worldview, as opposed to an explicit or implied Christian worldview.

Having been born of God's Spirit how would a Christian view a nation? And how can people holding this view from many a blunder free it?

Take any Western nation. Western cultures are Christianised cultures. Some more. Some less: a lot less! To be Christianised doesn't mean that everyone in the nation is Christian. It simply means that they are under the influence of the so-called Judeo-Christian ethic. In other words, the teaching of the Old and New Testaments, i.e., the Bible, permeates that culture – to a greater or a lesser extent.

Culture is religion externalised. Music, food, drink, mode of dress, politics, architecture, art *et al* are expressions of culture, of a nation's religion. That's why it is worth restating what we saw in an earlier quote articulated by John Eidsmoe regarding the overthrow of Scottish culture by the British after the Battle of Culloden,

> All forms of Scottish culture, including the playing of bagpipes, the wearing of the kilt, and the speaking of Gaelic, were banned.[53]

However, unlike the British establishment at the time of Bonnie Prince Charlie, Christianity does not destroy culture. Christianity influences culture for the better. The City of Glasgow's motto expresses this idea well: "Let Glasgow flourish by the preaching of Thy Word and the singing of Thy praise."

Using the Bible as its blueprint, Christianity transforms culture, making it more wholesome. Christianity helps nations think Christianly. Therefore, on account of its positive influence, Christianity frees nations from making many blunders!

---

[53] John Eidsmoe, *Historical and Theological Foundations of Law: Volume 2, Classical and Medieval*, (Expanded Second Edition, printed November 2016, Nordskog Publishing Inc., Ventura, California, 2016), 787.

Christianity influences nations primarily from the pulpit, i.e., from preaching. The Bible is expounded from cover to cover, which is to say that the Gospel is proclaimed and the Law is explained each Lord's Day from the pulpits of the faithful. As Jesus tells us, His church, with warning, that we are the salt and the light,

> You are the salt of the earth; but if the salt loses its flavor, how shall it be seasoned? It is then good for nothing but to be thrown out and trampled underfoot by men. You are the light of the world. A city that is set on hill cannot be hidden. Nor do they light a lamp and put it under a basket, but on a lampstand, and it gives light to all that are in the house. Let your light so shine before men, that they may see your good works and glorify your Father in heaven. Do not think that I came to destroy the Law or the Prophets. I did not come to destroy but to fulfil. For assuredly, I say to you, till heaven and earth pass away, one jot or one tittle will by no means pass from the law till all is fulfilled.[54]

The Gospel with the Law brings liberty to the people. The Law, properly understood and properly applied, enables the Christianised nation to retain its liberty. Healthy pulpit: Healthy nation.

Where the Gospel is stifled God's Law is flouted. By Gospel we mean the Good News that Jesus Christ died for sinners. By Law we mean the Ten Commandments that shows that all of us are sinners –

---

[54] Matthew 5:13-18 (NKJV)

in need of the Saviour of sinners, Jesus Christ. Not only does the preaching of God's Law expose us as sinners in need of salvation in Christ, but, (as well as showing Christians how to live their lives in demonstration of their gratitude to God for saving them), it also shows us how to restrain evil in our nation.

Christianity helps us to see the nation as God sees it and thus frees that nation from many a blunder!

Many pulpits in the West preach another gospel, which is not the Gospel. They preach what is known as the Social Gospel. The message of the Social Gospel has more to do with Marxism than the salvation of the individual by grace through faith in the saving work of Jesus Christ. Others preach a gospel that is devoid of God's Law. Indeed, they preach against the Law, as if the Ten Commandments were something evil, something to be rejected! Either way, the Gospel is robbed of its power. In this limp condition it cannot transform the individual and certainly not the nation! Says Joel McDurmon,

> Unless conservative Christians can present a forward-looking, optimistic vision for society, then they will continue to allow socialism and other unbiblical systems to succeed.[55]

Pray that God will raise up gifted preachers; preachers able to proclaim and explain the Gospel with the Law, so that the lives of the hearers will be transformed by its power, so that they will transform

---

[55] Joel McDurmon, *God versus Socialism: A Biblical Critique of the New Social Gospel*, (American Vision Press, Powder Springs, Georgia, 2009), 33.

the nations in which the live. So that their culture will be a Christian culture. Yes, God redeems individuals, but by an individual at a time, He eventually redeems whole nations! May your culture be Christian!

Jesus says,

> All authority has been given to Me in heaven and on earth. Go therefore and **make disciples of all the <u>nations</u>, baptising <u>them</u>** in the name of the Father and of the Son and of the Holy Spirit, **teaching <u>them</u> to observe all things that I have commanded you**…[56]

> Bottom line: Healthy pulpit: Healthy nation! Meanwhile back in America…

Are Trump Supporters Saviours of Western Civilization?

I'm not here to defend Donald Trump. He's a big boy and can take care of himself. However, as already noted, I fear for the West. President Trump is a real stick-in-the-spokes of the wheels of the Socialist/Progressive utopian agenda. The media (i.e., most of it), is the propaganda wing of this blight on Western civilization. "Fake News" IS propaganda, false propaganda. If all I did was watch fake news I fear that I would become a Trump hater too!

Regarding Leftist media political correctness, using her usual brand of humour, Ann Coulter writes,

---

[56] Matthew 28:18b-20a. (Emphasis mine.)

It's great living in America and having to interpret news stories as if we're reading *Pravda*...[57]

Don't miss the irony in Ann Coulter comparing America's "Free Press" to *Pravda*, the former official newspaper of the Communist Party. Ann Coulter goes on to say,

The *Chattanooga Times Free Press's* story on Vicente-Sapon's conviction was headlined "Illegal Alien Arrested for Incest, Child Rape, Kidnapping, and Sex Slavery." Just kidding! It was: "Man Guilty in Case of Human Smuggling." *Oh, and it was a MAN. How fascinating.* The *Free Press* never mentioned that the human smuggler was an illegal alien. That information was available only in the federal district court opinion dismissing Vicente-Sapon's motion to exclude his statements to the police of the grounds that the Spanish translator misunderstood him. But at least the *Free Press* reported the story. According to Nexis, it was the only news outlet to do so.[58]

Scotland had a beef against the mis-reporting (read "lies") of the BBC, (see e.g., G. A. Ponsonby's book "London Calling") during its famous

____

[57] Ann Coulter, *Adios, America!: The Left's Plan to Turn Our Country into a Third World Hellhole*, (Regnery Publishing, Washington. D.C., First paperback edition: 2016), 146.
[58] Ibid., 150.

Referendum. This is exactly how I see most of the media regarding President Trump. Fake! Spin! Lies! I just love the way Donald Trump pushes, nay, fights back. And so he should. Words matter because truth matters!

That's where my personal interest lies, i.e., in truth. It would be nice to get back to politics and the discussing of the same, aye, even heatedly, rather than listening to hysterical ranters who wouldn't recognize truth if it held a door open for them!

President Trump has given Western civilization at least some hope of survival. The Left's (conscious or unconscious) attempt at collapsing the system (i.e., Western Democracy) has itself collapsed on itself (for the moment).

Dialectical Materialism, with its Thesis, Antithesis and resultant Synthesis has been stalled by the people who elected Donald Trump. In other words, the *Thesis* is Capitalism. The *Antithesis* is Communism. And the hoped for resultant collapse of Capitalism would have been the *Synthesis*, i.e., Socialist Utopia, wherein, for the sale of your soul, the Government takes care of you cradle to grave. Simplistic analysis?

Sure, this is a simplistic view of the neo-Marxist Movement. But why complicate things? Western Democracy (including America) was on the verge of destruction by the Left, through its (Alinskian) demonizing and shouting-down anyone who did not hold its ideology. Many non-Lefties were afraid to speak their minds, lest they be vilified, thereby losing their jobs, business for businesses, etc.

Thank God for the privacy of the ballot-box, whereby those that the Political Correctness Movement had silenced, were given voice. In this instance ye olde Edmund Burke adage rang true, "The only thing necessary for the triumph of evil is for good men to do nothing." Good people voted. Democracy!

The press (most of it!) is the propaganda-wing of the Left. That is why President Trump (initially) bypasses the press by Tweeting his statements directly to his audience. News straight from the horse's mouth is better than its first going through the press's centrifuge. In other words, Trump-tweets take the spin out of his comments!

Trump launched his own social media platform, called *Truth Social*, in 2022. It is a free speech alternative to Twitter and Facebook etc, which groups took an anti-Trump stance, twisting his words and even banning him from their platforms. Elon Musk bought out Twitter and renamed it X, which helped to protect the cause of free speech. *Truth Social* arose on account of Trump being banned from social media platforms particularly in response to the "Fake Media" spin of the so called "January 6 Capitol riots", whereby many protestors, protesting the rigged election result, can be seen being given grand tours of the Capitol building by security guards and police. One protestor, Ashli Babbit, was fatally shot and killed by a security officer. Her family receiving almost a US $5 million settlement demonstrates the complexity of the issue. Many of the protestors were hunted down and imprisoned merely for the crime of "trespassing." To be sure, it was not one the Republican Party's supporters' finest moments. Riots never are. However, the media made it look like they had trashed the capitol and were out to murder everyone who disagreed with them, as opposed to merely protesting political injustice. Even the BBC's *Panorama* was in on the anti-Trump pile on, inflaming the public by cutting and splicing a videoed speech Trump made on 6th January 2021 addressing his supporters. It spliced two separate clips to make him say, "We're going to walk down to the Capitol… and I'll be there with you. And we fight. We fight like hell." Trump sued the BBC for $10 billion.

The electing of Donald Trump as President of the United States, (i.e., the big brother of the rest of the West) has given hope to the survival of Western civilization, including Australia. Just as the British Broadcasting Corporation was sprung for all its blatant and outright lying to the Scots, to sway them towards retaining the *status quo* Establishment in its Referendum, so the rest of the Western media, (the ABC, SBS in Australia etc., CNN, MSNBC, CBS *et al* in America) have been weighed in the scales of justice and have been found to be wanting! Dinesh D'Souza says,

> We cannot understand the tactics of the socialist left without penetrating its most powerful institution, the media, and that institution's staple product, fake news. The media is critical because it is the channel through which the American people get virtually all of their political information. Even Trump's Twitter account, which avoids the distorting filter of the media, must pass through

the channel of a digital media platform. Of the left's three big megaphones–academia, Hollywood and the media–the media is unquestionably the most important. Without the media, no one in America–not even critics of the media–has any comprehensive idea of what's going on.[59]

Freed from the shackles of a media that was shackled to the concrete blocks of Leftist ideology, such as Political Correctness, demonizing that which does not hold to Leftist ideology, we can now once more start talking about and actually debating issues.

Those speaking in favour of the issue? Say your piece. Those against? Let's hear you. We've sufficiently discussed the issue? Now let's put it to a vote. All those in favour? Against if any? The ayes (or the nays) have it. Thus, Western Democracy (but not Alt-Left ideology).

Marxism, just like Militant Islam, to make use of the analogy once more, is a square peg in a round hole. Neither fits into Western Democratic nations. Sure, they can be forced in with a hammer (and sickle or scimitar), but its end result is ugly, not utopia!

Marxism has an aversion to private property and private ownership (including private thoughts!). Ultimately this translates into an aversion of national borders. Likewise, Militant Islam doesn't believe in borders either. It wants to turn the whole earth into a Caliphate!

---

[59] Dinesh D'Souza, *United States of Socialism; Who's Behind it. Why it's Evil. How to Stop it*, (All Points Books, New York, 2020), 227-228.

I for one, am thankful that Lefty politics gave Donald Trump the presidency (twice!). Perhaps the Left will get back to working *with* the right (instead of against it) to build a better Western civilization, nation by nation, in which people are free as individuals under law, and free from needless government interference and intrusion, which interference and intrusion would be the case if we lived in the fabled Utopia of the Progressives/Socialists.

The Trump phenomenon which resulted in his (surprising to many) political success is due to the backfiring of the Left's continual demonization (see e.g., Saul Alinski's Rules for Radicals) of the Republican candidate.

For the Left (and some other Progressives) the general plan of attack is that you do not engage your opponent in discussing the "issues" but simply attack them by shouting him/her down by calling them names – Racist, fascist, misogynist, Islamophobe, homophobe, transphobe bigot etc., etc. Thus, like acid being thrown in a person's face, or turning a blowtorch on him/her, your opponent is inundated and blasted with vitriolic hate and hatred. Make no mistake, to demonize your opponent is to spread hate. This is supposed to set every "decent" person against your "sub-human" adversary. Trump's success is due to grass-roots people seeing the vacuity of this.

The more the media and the rest of Trump's opponents used these devious and ominous tactics and devices to try to belittle and demonize him (along with his "basket of deplorables" à la Hilary Clinton, not to mention the failed assassination attempts), the more his support-base expanded and increased, leading to winning both elections for him. Thus, the Political Correctness Movement accomplished Trump's presidency for him. How so? To labour the point, "the boy who cried wolf" springs to mind. When you keep on yelling "fire" when and where there is no fire people will switch off and stop listening to you. Anyone can check for themselves whether a thing is a fact or merely spin – by going to the primary source of the story and not relying on secondary sources like the media, for example. Or you can just sheepishly and naively accept what others say about their opponent.

There is a militant Leftist movement that styles itself by the name Antifa. Made up of many groups, such as anarchists, socialist and communists, they anarchistically protest everything and everyone they disagree with. Their protests are mostly violent. Apparently and ironically Antifa is supposed to mean anti-fascist! Says George Orwell,

> The word *Fascism* has now no meaning except in so far as it signifies 'something not desirable.' … Since you don't know what Fascism is, how can you struggle against Fascism? One need not swallow such absurdities as this, but one ought to recognize that the present political chaos is connected with the decay of language, and that one can probably bring about some improvement by starting at the verbal end. If you simplify your English, you are freed from the worst follies of orthodoxy.[60]

---

[60] George Orwell, *Politics and The English Language*, (Penguin Books, first published 1945, 2013), 8-9, 19-20.

President Trump uses a simplified English, albeit an American English, but nevertheless an English that people can easily understand. That is his appeal.

The bad news of the demonization-tactic is that, not only does your opponent get falsely smeared, but so do many others. The resultant collateral damage (of the failure of trying to demonize your opponent by false and/or way-over-the-top accusations) is that some people will inevitably believe the lies and use them to further their own ends – from bullying in the classroom to mass anarchistic riots in city streets where people are injured and property, including private property, is destroyed. Yes, and even try to rid the world of the one being falsely accused and smeared as a *fascist dictator* through assassination. Speaking of lies, in the following, Eric D. Butler alerts us to the ominous beliefs and furtive methods and tactics employed by the Communists. Says Butler,

> Over the recorded history of man there have been many attempts by some men to obtain complete power over all other men. But for the first time man is faced with a challenge by a power-seeking movement which claims that it is based upon a philosophy which can be used to demonstrate "scientifically" that murder, lying, deceit and stealing are but an aspect of Truth. According to the Communist philosophy of dialectical materialism, anything which advances Communism is therefore true. This statement will appear incredible to those

who know nothing about the "law" of dialectics as taught by the Communists. Dialectics is not some obscure subject which the non-Communist can safely ignore. Dialectics is a weapon of conquest in the hands of the dedicated Communist...

[Georg Wilhelm Friedrich] Hegel taught that the final idea was only reached through three stages. He termed the first stage *thesis*. This is the enunciation of the truth in the original idea. Now the *thesis* contains within itself its opposite, and Hegel termed the development of this the *antithesis*. The *antithesis* is not a mere negation of the *thesis*, but in fact must contain some truth because of its attack on error in the *thesis*. The next stage of development is the *synthesis*, which is the total of truth from both the *thesis* and *antithesis*. The *synthesis* then becomes the *thesis* of a new dialectical movement. Thus dialectical development can go on indefinitely. However, Communists do not like to face the question of why, if they really believe in the "law" of dialectics, they can accept the Communist State as the final stage of development in society![61]

Political Correctness hadn't/hasn't been thought through enough.

Meanwhile back to the planet earth...

---

[61] Eric. D. Butler, *"Dialectics" Communist Instrument for World Conquest*, (Melbourne, no date), 1-2, & 10.

Global Warming

I must admit that I was warming ever so slightly to the possibility of "Global Warming" way back when my wife asked me if I had noticed that they (whoever "they" are!) no longer seemed to be calling it "Global Warming" but were now calling it "Climate Change".

I guess the term "Climate Change" is a lot more encompassing (if not more accurate) than *ye olde* "Global Warming". For example, if the January temperature at the corner of Portage and Main in Winnipeg, Manitoba, Canada drops anywhere below the usual minus 40-degrees then it safely can be attributed to "Climate Change". Brilliant!

Mind you, now that I'm on to "their" scheming (as alluded to in "their" spin-doctoring use of terminology) I'm cooling somewhat in regard to "their" notion of "Global Warming". And then came "Climategate" with their misuse of (ice) hockey-stick graphs.

No doubt the Climate Status Quo deniers and sceptics will see the East Anglia University e-mails as inadmissible evidence in this whole so-called scientific debacle regarding the earth's mean climate. But regardless of how the irrefutable evidence was obtained, it was the smoking gun that killed the whole idea of Global Warming for me!

One Tim Flannery is an Australian "Climate Change" prophet of Doom. Yet none of his wild and fantastical "prophesies" (no more rain, rapidly rising sea-levels etc.) have come to pass. Old Testament prophets were to be stoned to death if any of their prognostications failed to materialise! Says an article in The Australian (note the year referred to),

> Tim Flannery, The Age, Oct 28, 2006, "There will be no Arctic icecap in the next five to 15 years … James Hanson, director of NASA's Goddard Institution, is arguably the world authority on climate change. He predicts that we have just a decade to avert a 25m rise of the sea."[62]

Sticks and stones may break my bones, but names will never hurt me! (I know, I know that the PC crowd actually believe that calling people names does indeed hurt, otherwise they wouldn't be calling non-Lefties "Nazi! Hitler! Fascist! Misogynist! Islamophobic! Homophobe! Bigot! etc., etc., etc.) However, before anyone calls me a "Climate Denier" (which sadly, in the minds of the Global Alarmists) is right up there with denying the Jewish Holocaust, I believe that the global temperature may be warming slightly. Is this slight warming caused by solar flares or burning fossil fuels or both? What difference does it make? Anything that we try to do about it has been proven to be negligible. This is one of the reasons why President Trump has pulled the USA out of the "Paris Agreement".

"Climate Change" scientists using data to make it say whatever they want it to say? This is right up there with that other great "scientific" sleight of hand, i.e., the molecules to man Theory of Evolution! The latter was and still is the slippery slope to the former.

---

[62] The Australian, Nov 28, 2018.

Okay, so you may disagree with the connection I'm drawing between the "sciences" of Evolutionary Theory and that of Climate Change Theory, but both are desperate to make their "evidence" fit their pet theories. That's unscientific in my book, (and in anyone's book).

Back in the day Britain's Prime Minister, Gordon Brown was calling those scientists who have not jumped on the "Global Warming" bandwagon, "Flat Earthers". O yeah! Sticks and stones may break my bones… But this also was and still is unscientific. One should not mix Leftist politics with science.

It seems to me that two things were going on. It was being touted as a fact that

    a) the global temperature was increasing
    b) the (supposed) global warming is man-made.

It's unscientific to call theories facts. It's also unscientific to ban peer reviews of those who disagree with the theory, (as is the case in regard to the molecules to man Theory of Evolution and now with the Theory of Climate Change).

Like BBC Scotland being the propaganda department of the British Establishment, as exampled in spinning its anti-Independence "fake news" during the Scottish Referendum debate, so the ABC (Australian Broadcasting Corporation) is the propaganda wing for the Left Down Under. It's tax-payer funded TV, Radio and online "news and discussions" programs are always about Lefties discussing and perhaps sometimes even disagreeing with other Lefties about issues that only Lefties see as important, such as Climate Change, the effect of

Climate Change on the Great Barrier Reef, LGBQI etc. The ABC's anti-Trump bias is embarrassing! But I digress, yet again.

Oh well, as I was with the "Global Cooling" fearmongering in the 70s, I was nearly warming to the idea of "Global Warming" (but still had a long way to go to embrace the idea that it was man made and that anything we can do will have any meaningful impact on its reduction). But that's all fallen by the wayside now. I'm now of the view that it's all a big hoax. It's mostly about wealth redistribution, as in Socialism! Is your country going to be swamped by rising sea-levels caused by Climate Change? Here! Have some of our nation's worker's hard-earned cash which we've relieved them of by unfair taxes, such as, taxes on carbon, breathing even! And if any of our taxpayers disagree with our Socialist ideals we'll just call them names. That will shut them up!

The issue of global warming is probably settled. The issue that it is manmade is still moot.

At the same time as people in hi-vis "yellow vests" were rioting in the streets of Paris over French President Macron's draconian "Carbon Tax", which is due to his adherence to the "Paris Accord", at the UN's Climate Change Summit in Katowice, Poland (November 2018), David Attenborough was saying,

> If we don't take action, the collapse of our civilsations and the extinction of much of the natural world is on the horizon… Right now we are facing a man-made disaster of global scale,

our greatest threat in thousands of years: climate change.[63]

Talk about scaring the kids! While all of this was going on, there were teachers who allowed their classes to attend a protest instead of school. On Friday, 30 November, 2018, these scared kids gathered in Brisbane city. Says ABC News in an article,

> Thousands of Australian students have defied calls by the Prime Minister to stay in school and instead marched on the nation's capital cities, and some regional centres, demanding an end to political inertia on climate change. Protests were held in Sydney, Brisbane, Perth, Coffs Harbour, Bendigo and other cities, as students banded together to pressure the Morrison Government in the lead-up to a federal election. "The politicians aren't listening to us when we try to act nicely for what we want and for what we need," said Castlemaine student Harriet O'Shea Carre. "So now we have to go to extreme lengths and miss out school."[64]

Do you hear that music playing in the background? It's Pink Floyd,

> We don't need no education
> We don't need no thought control
> No dark sarcasm in the classroom

---

[63] Evening Standard (on-line), 04 December 2018.
[64] ABC News (on-line), Friday 30 Nov 2018.

Teachers, leave them kids, alone
Hey Teacher! Leave us kids, alone!
All in all, it's just another brick in the wall
All in all, you're just another brick in the wall[65]

So, at the same time there was one lot protesting their President's unwavering adherence to "The Paris Agreement", we see another lot protesting their Prime Minister for not adhering to it enough! Who is right? Well, President Trump for pulling the U.S. out of the agreement. The Climate Change protests are all about unfair taxes. Macron listened to the Paris people who did not want the Paris Accord because it results in higher taxes, such as the fuel tax he tried to inflict on them. He reneged.

Al Gore-ithms

How can we talk about Global warming without mentioning the Prophet of Doom, Al Gore and his *Inconvenient Truth* propaganda movie? In 2006 Al Gore said that sea-levels would rise 20 feet. Denis T. Avery refers to this in the following,

> The study, "Snowfall-driven Growth in East Antarctic Ice Sheet Mitigates Recent Sea-level Rise" was led by Curt Davis of the University of Missouri, and reported in *Science* on June 24, 2005.
> Thickening ice in the Antarctic, in fact, is just about offsetting the meltwater being released from the edges of the Greenland ice sheet–

---

[65] Roger Waters & David Gilmour, Pink Floyd, *Another Brick in the Wall*.

which has also been thickening in its center. This leaves us with a global warming sea level gain of about 1.8 millimetres per year – or 4 inches per century. The rise has remained constant during the 20th century despite the moderate 0.6 degree C warming of the planet.

In the movie, a whole Antarctic ice sheet shatters on Gore's computer screen. In the real world, that isn't happening. It is only the Antarctic Peninsula – 2 percent of the continent's land area that sticks up toward the far-off equator–that is warming. It recently earned headlines by calving an ice flow as big as Rhode Island, not an unusual event.

But the East Antarctic ice sheet is more than 2,000 times bigger than Rhode Island, and the ice is two miles thick! John Stone of the University of Washington, reporting in *Science* on January 3, 2003 says the West Antarctic ice sheet has been retreating so slowly for the past 10,000 years that it still has not fully accommodated the end of the last Ice age, and apparently still has about 7,000 years of ice to melt – and the East Antarctic ice sheet is melting even more slowly than that.

So, Al Gore says Antarctic melting will suddenly raise the sea levels by 20 feet, and the experts say 4 inches per century."[66]

If we start with an ice-age, all are agreed that the planet is warmer now than then. But, what caused

[66] Denis T Avery, *Will Sea Levels Rise as Gore Predicts?* (Canada Free Press, Tuesday, July 11), 2006.

the great glacial icesheets to recede? This is where we enter the area of speculation. Likewise, when we discuss contemporary global warming, its rate and its causes. If we begin with the Ice-Age we will quickly see two opposing views emerge, viz., the Christian (or Biblical) perspective and the Uniformitarian. Let's call the former 'Creationist' and the latter 'Evolutionist', noting there're variables within both these worldviews.

Though believing that the earth is 4.5 billion years old, because of global warning, like a religious zealot, the Evolutionist believes that 'the end is nigh!' – if we do not do something. Panic! The Creationist? Well, the Creationist looks to God and His written Word. 'And a great windstorm arose, and the waves beat into the boat, so that it was already filling. But He [Jesus] was in the stern, asleep on a pillow. And they awoke Him and said to Him, 'Teacher, do You not care that we are perishing?' Then He arose and rebuked the wind, and said to the sea, 'Peace, be still!' And the wind ceased and there was a great calm. But He said to them, 'Why are you so fearful? How is it that you have no faith?' Mark 4:37-40. The Lord controls the weather. Consider Jonah fleeing from the presence of the LORD. 'But the LORD sent out a great wind on the sea, and there was a mighty tempest on the sea, so that the ship was about to be broken up' Jonah 1:4.

Examples could be multiplied. Does what we do affect the climate? You bet, but it's more moral than physical. We need to consider Noah's ark and the Flood. 'And God said to Noah, 'The end of all flesh has come before Me, for the earth is filled with violence through them; and behold, I will destroy them with the earth.'… All the fountains of the great deep were broken up, and the windows of heaven were opened. And the rain was on the earth forty days and forty nights' Genesis 6:13; 7:11b-12. As it was for the Egyptians chasing the Israelites, so it was in the global Deluge. The divided waters came together sandwiching man and beast across the earth. That is why we find millions of dead things that have been buried quickly in solidified sediment, including fossil fuels, i.e., coal, oil and gas reserves.

Post-Flood, primarily due to the ensuing soaring global humidity, centuries of heavy snowfalls caused the polar regions to greatly expand. Therefore, unlike the Uniformitarian/Evolutionist, who works off a timescale of billions of years, the Creationist looks to the ensuing effects of the global Flood some 4,300 years ago. The Ice-Age lasted for a few hundred years. Job, who lived before the time of Abraham, when speaking of snow and ice (not normal for his region), may be referring to the Ice-Age. 'The waters harden like stone, and the surface of the deep is frozen' Job 38:30. (E.g., see also Job 6:16; 9:30; 24:19; 37:6; 38:22,29.) That, in a nutshell, is the Creationist take on global warming.

Is the planet warming? Yes! Should we panic? No! Are fossil fuels the primary cause? No! If Western nations stopped using fossil fuels it would have minimal effect on the climate. Does God want us to be good stewards of His earth? Yes! 'Therefore, whether you eat or drink, whatever you do, do all to the glory of God' 1 Corinthians 10:31. Says Mark Levin,

Patrick Moore, Greenpeace cofounder and Canadian ecologist, testified before the United

States Senate that "there is 'little correlation' to support a 'direct causal relationship' between CO2 emissions and rising global temperatures. 'There is no scientific proof that human emissions of carbon dioxide are the dominant cause of the Earth's atmosphere over the past 100 years. If there were such a proof, it would be written down for all to see. No actual proof, as it is understood in science, exists.'" Moore "also criticized the UN's Intergovernmental Panel on Climate Change (IPCC) for claiming 'it is extremely likely' that human activity is the 'dominant cause' for global warming, noting that 'extremely likely' is not a scientific term. Moore warned the statistics presented by the IPCC are not the result of mathematical calculations of statistical analysis, and may have been 'invented' to support the IPCC's 'expert judgement.'"[67]

I like the idea of solar-power. I've stuck twenty solar-panels on the roof of my suburban home. It's great to run my hot tap, my dishwasher, my washing machine, my outdoor spa, my TV, all my electricity during the day for virtually nothing. But then at night it gets dark and I don't get any free electrical power! And sometimes even during the day it gets cloudy and I don't get any free electricity! The solar-batteries are a bit too expensive at the moment to make it worth my while getting one for power storage. Also, I don't believe the government should use the taxpayer's

---

[67] Mark R. Levin, *Unfreedom of the Press*, (Threshold Editions, New York, NY, 2019), 126-7.

money to subsidise these types of things. And governments should certainly not be involved in subsidising "renewables", such as windfarms. This makes government a business competitor with an unfair advantage rather than the business referee.

On a lighter side (excuse the pun), a short note on what I call "greenie lightbulbs", you know, the ones that when you flick the switch they take a moment to come on? These "greenie bulbs" allege that a 20 watt or whatever bulb is the equivalent of *ye olde* 100 watt bulb. These new bulbs remind me of a humorous Spike Milligan anecdote of the time he was joining his Regiment,

> "You're not Milligan are yew?"
> "Actually I am."
> A beam of sadistic pleasure spread over his face.
> "We've been waiting for yew!" he said, pushing me ahead of him with his stick. He drove me into what was D Battery Office. The walls once white were now thrice grey. From a peeling ceiling hung a forty watt bulb that when lit made the room darker.[68]

Meanwhile back in Western Civilisation...

The Empire Fights Back

It looked really grim for Western civilization. One could just about smell the smoke of burning national flags and hear strains of Black Sabbath's "War

---

[68] Spike Milligan, *Adolf Hitler, My Part in His Downfall*, (Penguin Books, Kindle Edition, 2012).

Pigs" playing as images of raging mobs with pitchforks and flaming torches tearing down statues were flashed on walls of crumbling and bombed-out buildings to mark the success of "Earth Day". Says Baptist Theologian James White,

> There was a day when we deplored mobs and those who would join them. Mobs do not promote careful thought, deep consideration. They inflame emotion, and thrive on lies. Rome fell into mob rule toward the end. We are accelerating in our downward spiral.[69]

It was in the midst of the chaotic mob-rule takeover that a bolt of hope shot out of the blue! Donald Trump is hard to define. Presently he is constantly being attacked left, right and centre, but he's still standing. Why? Well, for a start, the attacks are making him stronger! (not least of all in the eyes of his supporters). It's like a martial arts' expert using his opponent's force of momentum to his own advantage. I'm more Star Trek-ian than a Star Wars-ian, but the Donald, as it were, is using The Force! Obviously, this would be a great quality for any president to have. Resilience. Trump seems to sap his critics of their power. Nay, like coal to a power-station, they are actually feeding raw materials into The Donald's power-grid! How so?

The West has two lethal enemies working hand in hand at the moment, viz., Islamic Terrorism and Political Correctness. (That, I have to say, is indicative of where we are in the West. But notice that I did NOT

---

[69] James White, comment on Twitter.

say that ALL Islamists are terrorist, nor am I suggesting this!) The latter (i.e., PC) means that the Left (primarily) does not allow you even to talk about the former. It's just "terrorism". Talk about the blind leading the blind, whether the terrorism is Presbyterian or Islamist is neither here nor there, but only for those who religiously follow the false religion of Political Correctness.

One is left to wonder if there are Presbyterians walking around with bomb-vests that we need to be watching out for! Ludicrous! The PC extremists simply spray with vitriol anyone who tries to talk about the-elephant-in-the-room, i.e., Militant Islam. This kind of insanity is exactly what is feeding energy into the Trump power-grid.

The Left, along with the so-called "Establishment Republicans", attack him with the same failed and hackneyed tactics of trying to paint him as some sort of Racist, Islamophobic Misogynist, Nazi, Fascist etc. Talk about "the boy who cried 'wolf'"? Surely the Trump opponents are not unaware that this just strengthens and adds to Trump's vast following? This is exactly what the Trump movement is reacting against. For this kind of attempt at *ad hominem* character assassination through demonization is the application of Political Correctness. Confused? Let me explain further.

Politicians use "guarded speech" and "careful language", which is to say that they end up saying nothing of substance by using Political Correctness to avoid attack from political opponents, also including the media. Donald Trump does the opposite. He talks as a "normal" human being would talk about "normal" issues facing the world today, e.g., Islamic Terrorism; Border Control and the interrelation of these to each other among other things. The Left wishes to red-paint him as Islamophobic and Racist etc. And the so-called "Establishment Republicans" portray him as "un-presidential". They condescendingly wish for Trump to become more "presidential". However, what the Trump supporters hear the "Establishment" saying by these actions is that Trump needs to become more Politically Correct – with its attendant guarded speech where no one really knows what you are saying exactly. However, they all forget that in the age of the Internet anyone can replay what Trump actually has said, and not what the Left wants you to think he said! Yes, and Trump's following <u>can</u> be bothered looking these things up on the Web, and do! Thus, the Trump numbers keep on being added to and his opponents are left wearing the emperor's new clothes.

You may not agree with some of the methods Donald Trump uses to defend himself, his party, and, even truth itself. However, you have to agree that his method of communicating through tweets and *Truth Social* is genius in these days when reporters no longer report the news but instead comment on it. They have become commentators rather than reporters.

First off, Trump is attacked for using Twitter and constantly Tweeting. Un-presidential! Second off, Trump is attacked for the content of his Tweets! Third off, they find Donald Trump and his tweets offensive. But, like Mr Ed, all it is is words coming straight from the horse's mouth, for which those of us who wish to know what he really said, (i.e., without the Leftist spin or Socialist filter), are truly thankful.

The Leftist media is Chinese whispers on steroids. But don't take my word for it. See for yourself. Obviously, John Cassidy is no friend of President Trump. Says Cassidy,

> Trump has attempted to delegitimize the entire fact-based press in the eyes of his opponents.[70]

Let's put the brakes on here before we go any further. "Delegitimize the entire fact-based press"? Really? Is this statement fact-based? Let's read the rest of the quote to see if that is what The Donald is actually saying. The Cassidy quote continues,

> "Stick with us," he [i.e., President Trump] said in a speech last week. "Don't believe the crap you see from these people, the fake news … What you're seeing and what you're reading is not what's happening." George Orwell gets quoted too liberally these days, but, as the national security expert David Priess pointed out, these statements were Orwellian in the extreme. ("The party told you to reject the evidence of your eyes and ears. It was their final, most essential command.") And, judging by Trump's steady approval ratings and the large crowds at his rallies, many people are willing to take him at his word.[71]

---

[70] John Cassidy, *The New Yorker*, How to Counter Donald Trump's War on the Media, August 3, 2018.
[71] Ibid.

As you can clearly see in the above, the grandiose statements being made in this quote clearly are not fact-based. It is over-the-top rhetoric. It is anti-Trump propaganda.

Cassidy, in his article, wishes to convince his readership that Trump is at odds with the *entire* media, or as he calls it, "the entire fact-based press". Where has Trump attempted to delegitimize the legitimate press? It is only "the crap" you see from these people, the "fake news" that Trump rightfully is delegitimizing. Big difference! In Scotland, to say the same thing as Trump, they might say, "Half the lies they tell are not true!" Who? The fake news, the people who espouse crap, that's who! As Francois Rabelais and William Shakespeare are reputed to have said, "Tell the truth and shame the devil." As Thomas Jefferson is reputed to have said, "Honesty is the first chapter in the book of wisdom." As Almighty God has said, "Thou shalt not bear false witness." Says Mark Levin,

> President Trump does not pose a threat to freedom of press…
> Newsrooms and journalists are not imperiled by the current president.
> There are no known sedition-act efforts attacking speech and press freedom; no executive orders imprisoning reporters and shuttering newspapers; no FCC actions against broadcast stations; no unprecedented criminal charges against media organizations or reporters; no omnipresent propaganda operations; etc.

Nonetheless, the constant media refrain, whether from journalists or editorialists, trying to convince the American people of a demonstrably false narrative – that President Trump has launched an unprecedented battering on freedom of the press, thereby undermining the credibility of the institution of a free press and the First Amendment with the public – is media propaganda *and* a media-concocted pseudo-event. Unfortunately, too much of what the public reads, hears, and sees from the Democratic party-press fits this description.[72]

Speaking of speaking the truth, it has been said that in the Union of Soviet Socialist Republics that even road maps could not be trusted let alone the Soviet press. Who wants to live in a world like that? Certainly not Trump voters – "judging by Trump's steady approval ratings and the large crowds at his rallies, many people are willing to take him at his word." They hear his word at his rallies and they read his word in his Tweets. They do not get it from "fake news". By the U.S.S.R.'s use of "fake-maps" one is reminded of what Spike Milligan says happened to him during the war years, "We were marched to a secret destination on the coast known only to us, and the enemy."[73]

---

[72] Mark R. Levin, *Unfreedom of the Press*, (Threshold Editions, New York, NY, 2019), 116.
[73] Spike Milligan, *Adolf Hitler, My Part in His Downfall*, (Penguin Books, Kindle Edition, 2012).

The Trump phenomenon is a movement against controlled-thought commonly known as Political Correctness, i.e., "mind-control". Trump followers are ecstatically emboldened that the president is not a politician. They do not want a politician in power, or what is known as a "career politician". President Trump is none of this. He speaks plainly, perhaps a little too plainly. That's what gets him in trouble. He sounds like a businessman, a businessman from Queens, New York. That's exactly what he is and that's exactly what his supporters have got.

It's time for an Orwellian quote. Says George Orwell,

> The great enemy of clear language is insincerity. When there is a gap between one's real and one's declared aims, one turns as it were instinctively to long words and exhausted idioms, like a cuttlefish squirting out ink. In our age there is no such thing as 'keeping out of politics'. All issues are political issues, and politics itself is a mass of lies, evasions, folly, hatred and schizophrenia. When the general atmosphere is bad, language must suffer.[74]

No party talking points from The Donald. No political smokescreens. No opaque use of language and phrases. Sure, he may at times use some garbled verbiage, but it's never verballed garbage. He says what he says when he was running for president. He

---

[74] George Orwell, *Politics and The English Language*, (Penguin Books, first published 1945, 2013), 15.

says what he means and means what he says. That's why his followers voted for him. His opponents hate him because they understand what he is saying.

To his followers Trump represents the removal of that which has shackled free speech in America and indeed the rest of the West for far too long. Says David Van Gend,

> Remember John Milton's cry to the English Parliament in 1644: "Give me the liberty to argue freely according to conscience, above all liberties." Free speech, free argument, is at the heart of a self-governing society, and yet that liberty is being constricted throughout the developed world in the name of a new and bogus 'right not to be offended'. The greatest free-speech warrior of the West, Canadian writer Mark Steyn, speaks from experience: "In Canada, I committed the crime of 'offending' certain approved identity groups. And there is no defense to that: truth, facts, evidence are all irrelevant. If someone's 'offended', that's that: You're guilty." Thanks to Steyn's magnificent push-back against the Canadian 'human rights' establishment, the Canadian Parliament repealed the vilification law under which he was harassed. In Australia that remains unfinished business.[75]

---

[75] David Van Gend, *Stealing from a Child: The Injustice of 'Marriage Equality'*, (Connor Court Publishing Party Ltd, 2016).

Speaking of Canadians, says Spike Milligan of the time he played in a band in the army during the war,

> Music has strange effects on drunks: one lunatic ripped open his battle-dress, pointed to a scar on his chest, and shouted "Dunkirk! you bloody coward." He had a face made from red plasticine by a child of three, that or his parachute didn't open… A fight broke out with the Canadians. They were all massive.
> "How do you get such huge men?" I asked one.
> "We go into the forest, shake the trees and they fall out," he said.
> A worried officer rushed up.
> "Can you play 'The Maple Leaf Forever'?"
> "No sir, after an hour I get tired."
> "You're under arrest," he said.[76]

Trump politics is an uprising against Political Correctness. The more the Left and the "Establishment Republicans" use it to try to stop him, the more power they give to Donald Trump and his vast army of believers.

President Donald Trump is the beginning of the downfall of Political Correctness. He has exposed the soft underbelly of all enemies of individual freedom, be they Islamist, Socialist (and its attendant spooky and creepy spectre, i.e., Communism). Use Alinsky's Rules for Radicals on President Trump by calling him names, and he'll retaliate and hit you back twice as hard. Of course, the "Fake News" will only

---

[76] Spike Milligan, *Adolf Hitler, My Part in His Downfall*, (Penguin Books, Kindle Edition, 2012).

give half the story and will never let its viewers know President Trump is merely responding to being called a name or being lied about. Says Michael Youssef,

> Whenever you take in news, remember that the so-called main stream media or legacy media – Reuters, the AP, CNN, ABC, CBS, NBC, NPR, the BBC, *The New York Times*, *The Washington Post*, *The Guardian*, and so forth – are all part of the Omnicause, the Red-Green Alliance. The far-left media is fully allied with Hamas and other Islamist groups, no matter what crimes they commit. Why? Because the media shares the Islamists' hatred for Western civilization.[77]

Meanwhile back to the Bible…

Addressing Political Correctness

I would like to address, albeit briefly, the whole idea of Political Correctness (PC). To be sure, there no doubt has been some benefits from this once upon a time well-meaning movement. I won't try to list any of those benefits here lest we, to use a mixed metaphor, get side-tracked with red herrings.

By-the-way, Political Correctness is a red herring used by the political Left to distract the un-attentive to what is really going on. It's not about racial equality and equality for women, jobs for the workers, welfare for the handicapped or any such like thing. It

---

[77] Michael Youssef, *An Unholy Alliance: How Progressivism Brought About an Islamist Invasion*, (Ascaine Press, Nashville, TN, 2026), 159.

has become a political weapon. However, it's really just Saul kicking against the goads. "Why do the nations rage, and the people plot such a vain thing? The kings of the earth set themselves, and the rulers take counsel together, against the LORD and against His Anointed, saying, 'Let us break Their bonds in pieces and cast away Their cords from us'" Psalm 2:1-2. Was this a red herring? No! But I did digress…

The idea of PC I'd like to address is that of what I shall call Political Correctness Extremism (PCE). PCE is a tool, nay, a weapon used by Progressives, if not to silence any opposition to their socialistic utopian dreams for society, at least to put that opposition on the defensive. In other words, PCE is a full-frontal attack on any and all honest discussion of any social issue. And so, it has become, that to oppose the Progressive view on any subject is to declare oneself to be immoral, cruel, greedy, intolerant and (fill in the rest with all the usual prefixes) phobic etc., etc., etc.

The Parable of the Good Samaritan might be useful to illustrate how Progressives use the old "bait and switch" tactic to further their political ends. Jesus told the Good Samaritan Parable to answer the question, "Who is my neighbour?" "In reply Jesus said: 'A man was going down from Jerusalem to Jericho, when he was attacked by robbers. They stripped him of his clothes, beat him and went away, leaving him half dead.'" Luke 10:29b-30. In the story, it was the Good Samaritan who really went out of his way to help the wounded man.

However, to the Progressive mind fixated on his/her version of cultural utopia it is not the half dead man who needs most help, it's the robbers who nearly killed him! And so the narrative becomes about how society has failed these people that they should need to resort to robbery! If only society had looked after them, they wouldn't have needed to resort to such desperate measures! These robbers were no doubt raised in a low socio-economic backwater with no opportunities. However, those who wish to talk about the actual issue, (i.e., that of an innocent man being robbed and sadistically beaten near to death) are shouted down as not caring about the terrible (they may even throw in the word "Capitalist") society that caused these poor underprivileged people to become robbers in the first place.

PCE has a narrative attached to it: Socialism. Like the proverbial square peg in a round hole, Socialism does not fit into Western civilization, i.e., what used to be called Christendom. Now, to really drive home the point, i.e., the whole point being made throughout this book, to be sure, with a lot of pounding hammers and noisy hammering, a square peg may be forced into a round hole – but the end result always and ever will look ugly!

The Progressive narrative is about driving home that square peg – regardless. Therefore, the things that made the West great, such as those Biblical teachings, those well-rounded tried and true Western things, such as Capitalism, Banking, Private Property, Free Market, Free Speech etc., become points of friction as the square peg of socialism is hammered home. Thus, PCE works hard to put those things that the West was won by in a bad light. Shady! So, instead of lifting the half dead man or woman out of the gutter and helping him or her to get on his or her feet, the story becomes about socially engineering a society in which people will not have to become robbers.

In this world, i.e., the world of Political Correctness Extremism (PCE), those who are brave enough, for example, to talk about *punishing* robbers are viewed as callous. Rehabilitation is the new order of the day. Murderous robbers are now the victims and the person beaten and robbed of his money was a Capitalist who, quite frankly, deserved everything he got! He had it coming.

All of this might sound a bit over the top rhetoric to some more moderate Progressives. However, one only needs to consider the events that took place in Paris, London, Melbourne and many other places to see the truth of what I say. The story is not about destroying ISIS and/or bringing justice to its members, i.e., *punishment*. Rather, thanks to PCE it is about everyday people in the West being lectured by Progressives and called bigots, racists, Islamophobes, phobics for daring to call ISIS *Islamic*! Thus, the injured, instead of having their wounds bandaged, are further beaten-up! Militant Islam attacks us physically and PCE Progressivism attacks us verbally. It is a joint attack on Western values! Either way, attacked from within and attacked from without, the West is doomed. The story has become all about the attackers having their pound of flesh, their utopia. Says Michael Youssef,

> Although the rape-gang crisis in Great Britain has been exposed, it has not been solved… The politically correct dogmas of the secular left

still compel officials to ignore child rape, torture, and even murder *if* these crimes are committed by Muslims. The officials worry more about being called 'racists' than they care about the destruction of innocent young lives… Progressives will do anything to prove how 'enlightened' and 'inclusive' they are. Progressives are scared to death of being labelled 'Islamophobic' and so, out of cowardice, and an obsession of 'political correctness,' join forces with the jihadists who seek to destroy us.[78]

If you are wondering what neo-Marxist Progressivism, i.e., being "Woke", has in common with radical Islam, it has to do with how dialectical materialism is supposed to progress through the collapse (brought on by revolution) of the present political system after which the Socialist utopia apparently draws nearer through the synthesis. Let's say that the Christian influence throughout the West is the *thesis*, the establishment, and the *antithesis* is the antiestablishment – as displayed by Islam and Socialism (both of which are clearly anti-Christian, though some Christians have been fooled into believing that Socialism expresses the teaching of the Bible!). When the present (Christian) establishment has been overturned, what emerges is the new *thesis*. This, apparently, is progress! Thus, Progressive dialectical materialism.

---

[78] Michael Youssef, *An Unholy Alliance: How Progressivism Brought About an Islamist Invasion*, (Ascaine Press, Nashville, TN, 2026), 26, 53.

Why do Marxists of all shades so willingly align themselves with Muslims? Says Paul Kengor of Atheist Karl Marx, "Sure, Muslims believed in God and that, to Marx, was a bad thing, but at least they were against Christians. They had that redeeming quality."[79] The old proverb, "My enemy's enemy is my friend" rings true here. It's like the Pharisees and the Sadducees burying the hatchet in a team effort to destroy Jesus.

(Are you ready for one final use of the "square peg" analogy?) Islamism is the square peg. Progressivism is the hammer. The West is the round hole. Please stop hammering. You're hurting us, nay, you're destroying us! But isn't that the point of the extreme Left, i.e., to bring down the West? It's an unholy alliance.

According to a pre-election Scottish edition of the English Daily Telegraph, it flagged the following under the headline – ***Do not vote, it's a sin...*** It said,

> Muslims are intimidated in the street. Some Muslims were told not to vote while others were allegedly ordered by spiritual leaders to back Labour as Tower Hamlets became the centre of election controversy yesterday. Two types of leaflet were distributed in Tower Hamlets [east London]. One displayed the words 'Don't vote' and '#StayMuslimDontVote'. It also read: 'None have the right to legislate except Allah.' The

---

[79] Paul Kengor, *The Devil and Karl Marx: Communism's Long March of Death, Deception, and Infiltration*, (TAN Books, Gastonia, North Carolina, 2020), 62-3.

other read: 'Warning. Voting for man-made law is Shirk [idol worship] associated with Allah.'

As we see above, during the lead up to Britain's General Election (May 7, 2015) some Muslims were urging other Muslims not to vote. These "Don't vote" type of Muslims don't sound that much different to many present day "Christians" who have come under the influence of Anabaptist theology with its attendant Pietism that is stifling Christianity's influence in the world. "[Jesus] said, "To what shall I liken the kingdom of God? It is like leaven, which a woman took and hid in three measures of meal till it was all leavened" Luke 13:20-21. E.g., the Amish and the Mennonites have turned their backs on society and have no Christian influence whatsoever apart from being cultural curiosities. Then there are others, such as Antinomians,[80] who think that the Ten Commandments have nothing to do with Christians!

Then there are others who don't believe in the following use of the Law as stated by RC Sproul,

> A second purpose for the law is the restraint of evil. The law, in and of itself, cannot change human hearts. It can, however, serve to protect the righteous from the unjust. Calvin says this purpose is 'by means of its fearful denunciations and the consequent dread of punishment, to curb those who, unless forced, have no regard for rectitude and justice.' The

---

[80] Antinomianism is comprised of two Greek words meaning against law.

law allows for a limited measure of justice on this earth, until the last judgment is realized.[81]

Then there are those who believe there are only Nine Commandments. They remove the Fourth Commandment of the Decalogue, the one regarding the Christian Sabbath, i.e., the Lord's Day.

Anyway, I've shortened to bumper-sticker size what the Presbyterian Robert Lewis Dabney says somewhere – here's the bumper-sticker, "Healthy Pulpit, Healthy Nation." We hear very little about God's Law from the pulpits and that is why the West is crumbling. As the West continues to implode, Socialism with its attendant Atheism and Islam with its attendant Sharia, is rushing in filling the void. Says Gary DeMar regarding the American context,

> The Left continues to attack Christians for their faith and yet says nothing about Islamists who do not believe in a jurisdictional separation between church and faith [sic. State?] (as Christians do). In fact, Democrats continue to vote for Muslims and put them in office. Democrats will give Islamists the rope with which they will hang us.[82]

The Irishwoman and great singer, Senéad O'Connor, who had a Roman Catholic background, seems now to be the epitome of the marriage between

---

[81]RC Sproul.

[82] Gary DeMar, "Rapture" thinking and political paralysis, The American Vision, Jan 7, 2019.

the Left and Islam. She had gone from shaving her head, and from publicly ripping pictures of popes, to covering her head with an Islamic hijab and calling herself Shahada (or is it Magda?) Davitt after converting to Islam. There was, of course, nothing wrong with her exercising her (Western) freedom to do this. However, it is the fact that we are rapidly losing our Western freedoms that most concerns me. Says Australian Presbyterian minister Graham Nicholson,

> It is not surprising then that where Calvin's Institutes [of the Christian Religion] were read and understood, society took on a distinctively Christian ethos quite different from that furthered by Medieval Catholicism. There was a balance between liberty and authority which preserved from the poles of tyranny and anarchy and which encouraged individual liberty and social responsibility. Those were "Protestant" lands. They are also the lands which have been responsible for so much of the social stability and prosperity of "the West" for the last 300 years. As the West now rapidly and foolishly turns away from its Biblical and Calvinist heritage, it will lose that which has made it distinctive, and the world will lose something very special. Instead of real blessing we will be left with the illusion of wisdom and a *"semblance of righteousness"* where anyone who stands for God will likely be considered a trouble-maker and a nuisance.[83]

---

[83] Rev. Graham Nicholson.

Bottom line? Christians need to get educated on what the *whole* Bible teaches! Then we will again be an influence for good on this earth. Why? Because "The earth is the LORD's, and all its fullness, the world and those who dwell therein" Psalm 24:1.

Antinomianism is as much an enemy of Christianity as Islam's Sharia Law. The West needs to return to the foundations it was built on, i.e., God's Moral Law as expressed in Ten Commandments in all their applications.

"For out of Zion shall go forth the law, and the word of the LORD from Jerusalem. He shall judge between the nations, and rebuke many people; they shall beat their swords into plowshares, and their spears into pruning hooks; nation shall not lift up sword against nation, neither shall they learn war anymore" Isaiah 2:3a-4.

My old theological professor actually had the following bumper-sticker on his car's bumper: "God's Law or Chaos."[84]

Meanwhile back to Christians and politics…

Socialism Unmasked

"She'll be right mate!" is Australian vernacular for the postmodernist "whatever!", which was a popular saying when I lived in Canada. When it comes to politics, both reek of complacent laidback-ness.

---

[84] See also Francis Nigel Lee, *God's Ten Commandments: Yesterday, Today, Forever,* (Nordskog Publishing Inc., Ventura, California, 2007).

Even among Christians there is debate as to whether identifiably Christian political parties are preferred to the usual atheist/socialist ones or even those conservative parties that espouse policies a lot of with which many Christians can agree. Surely Christians ought to form political parties based on the teaching of the Bible regarding life and politics. For, Scripture says, "Keep your heart with all diligence, for out of it *spring* the issues of life" (Prov. 4:23). Therefore, in light of this "qué será, será" laissez-faire approach to life and its issues, how can one expect civil disobedience from Christians? How should Christians respond when governments clearly overstep their God-given authority and start to lord it over the people? "She'll be right mate" or active obedience to God? The general principle all Christians are to follow is summed up in this verse, "Peter and the *other* apostles answered and said: 'We ought to obey God rather than men'" (Acts 5:29).

One only has to consider the so-called COVID-19 government authoritarianism and downright totalitarianism that took place in many western countries during the "Pandemic" in 2020-22 and beyond. In Australia the socialistic state and federal governments locked people in their homes, wouldn't let Australian residents return from overseas, nor allow interstate travel. Face masks were insisted upon by even those slightly less authoritarian states. Churches were not permitted to congregate, and when things lightened up a little, first, they were not allowed to sing praises to God even while wearing masks. Only family members could sit together, if not too many! And 'social distancing' became a thing. No golf! No kids playing in the park! No handshakes permitted and lots of hand cleaner available. Elderly people died alone, with loved ones not permitted to visit. Funerals could only be attended by a handful of people. All for what?

Then came Covid-shot police. People were ostracized for not getting the jab. Whistle blowers were silenced. Doctors and nurses lost their jobs for not conforming to the globalist/socialist narrative imposed by totalitarian/authoritarian governments. The authorities were informed by members of the public "dobbing in" their neighbours on hotlines designed just for that! Unfortunate for those whose name already is Karen, but a "Karen" became a derogative appellation affixed to any covid busybody. (See 2 Thess. 3:11; 1 Pet. 4:15.) Police in some states were seen smashing members of the public's faces to the ground for not wearing/improperly wearing their government-approved masks!

Governments controlled the media narrative. The public was not even allowed to discuss the issue of COVID-19. "False information" notices appeared on social media whenever anyone attempted to address the issue and related issues. Posts were blocked. Free speech was reduced to whispers while looking over one's shoulder.

Then came the negative bodily reactions against whatever was being injected into the masses. Reports of shingles, reactions from paralysis to death and everything in between. Again, governments would not allow any public discussion of this important issue.

We didn't know whether it was germ-warfare from a manufactured virus in Wuhan in China through "gain of function" (a phrase that entered the public's vocabulary), or something to do with infected bats and/or pangolins from a Chinese "wet market". Confusion reigned as Australians began wondering if their old adage "she'll be right mate!" was actually going to cover their present demise. People panicked! Some got many more "booster shots" to combat the virus, while others refused to get, even if they already had one, any more jabs. Distrust of government set in. "Big-Pharma" was viewed with great suspicion. Had they even tested their products, the stuff that they were being paid to manufacture and the authoritarian governments were insisting that the public have at least two jabs followed by many boosters? The short answer is that the public were being used as 'Guinea pigs'. In the 1960s the hippies voluntarily took 'experimental drugs' in a foolish attempt to expand their minds. In the 2020s governments forced members of the public to take experimental drugs on pain of loss of job and/or loss of face in society to the point of being treated as anarchists.

Governments made daily announcements on television reporting how many covid cases there were, leaving the public confused as to whether people were dying *with* covid or actually dying *from* covid. Every hospital death, it seemed, was a covid death, whether the person presently had the flu or some terminal illness.

Yes, the mask of Socialism slipped and exposed a face pock-marked with totalitarianism and authoritarianism, its slightly milder form. Neither of which are the Bible's view of civil government. (See e.g., Rom. 13:1-7; Titus 3:1; 1 Pet. 2:13-14.) Clearly, many federal and state governments in western nations overstepped their boundaries. They refused to stay in their lanes and interfered in the equally sovereign but connected spheres of family and church. Some even pushed their nation's constitution aside and handed over authority to health departments, many of whom, like "helicopter parents", wrapped joe-public in cotton wool and bubble wrap and locked them in their room. "Safety first!" is the mantra of a nanny state, aka Socialiam.

In 1644 Scottish Presbyterian minister, Samuel Rutherford, published a book called Lex Rex (Latin for The Law is King) advocating the rule of law, limited government, and the right to resist tyrannical rulers. Theologian, philosopher, apologist, and Presbyterian minister Francis Schaeffer wrote,

> Civil disobedience is, of course, a very serious matter and it must be stressed that Rutherford was the very opposite of an anarchist. In Lex Rex he does not propose armed revolution as an automatic solution. Instead, he sets forth the appropriate response to interference by the state in the liberties of the citizenry.

> Specifically, he stated that if the state deliberately is committed to destroying its ethical commitment to God then resistance is appropriate.[85]

Clearly, civil disobedience was called for during the totalitarian state's 'war games' practice run, aka the "Pandemic". Though pockets of resistance were to be found here and there, Christianity failed miserably! "She'll be right mate" is unbiblical. It is antibiblical! Schaeffer also wrote,

> The civil government, as all of life, stands under the law of God. In this fallen world God has given us certain offices to protect us from the chaos which is the natural result of that fallenness. But when *any office* commands that which is contrary to the Word of God, those who hold that office abrogate their authority and they are not to be obeyed. And that includes the state.[86]

If ever there was a time to form outwardly Christian governments, surely it is now? However, to counter socialist totalitarianism we need Christian governments built on more than one or two issues such as abortion and/or feeding the poor and clothing the

---

[85] The Complete Works of Francis A Schaeffer; A Christian Worldview, Volume 5, A Christian Worldview of the West, (Crossway Books, Wheaton, Illinois, 1982), 475.
[86] Ibid., 468.

needy. We need a contemporary Abraham Kuyper who was Prime Minister of the Netherlands from 1901 to 1905. His political party was called the *Anti-Revolutionist Party*. He implemented a system of "sphere sovereignty" among the different departments of government. This system has since through time and debate been perfected. There a three main spheres in a nation, viz, Family, Church, and State. Like each Person in the Godhead, each has its own sphere of authority under God but they are interconnected and must therefore look out for the other spheres without encroaching on their authority. Like Olympic swimmers, each sphere must stay in its own lane and operate therein without interfering with its neighbour.

COVID-19 was an exercise in government interference. It was when Socialism was totally unmasked.

Meanwhile back to the Bible again…

Everything in Common?

"All the believers were together and had everything in common" Acts 2:44.

Some misuse this verse in an attempt to justify Socialism and its ultimate goal, i.e., Communism. Socialism is another name for wealth redistribution, i.e., other people's wealth, by the State. We often hear that Socialism has never properly been tried in any country, that it just needs an opportunity to be done right. Apart from it being an unbiblical system, redistribution of wealth is stealing.

Earlier, we mentioned the much-maligned Prime Minister of Great Britain, Margaret Thatcher.

She had much to say about Socialism. E.g., "The problem with socialism is that sooner or later you run out of everyone else's money." And "No theory of government was ever given a fairer test or a more prolonged experiment in a democratic country than democratic socialism received in Britain. Yet it was a miserable failure in every respect... To cure the British disease with socialism was like trying to cure leukemia with leeches." And "The real case against socialism is not its economic inefficiency, though on all sides there is evidence of that. Much more fundamental is its basic immorality."

It should be noted that State and Government are not synonymous. The three main sovereign spheres of any nation are Family, Church, and State, within each of which is its own form of government, viz, parents (Eph. 6:1-4), elders (Titus 1:5-9), and civil rulers (Rom. 13:1-7).

First, let us notice some obvious things from this verse as they refer to the early church at that particular time.

Note that it is talking about a community of believers, i.e., a group of Christians: "All the *believers* were together." Therefore, because it is talking about believers, it is not talking about a nation's government taxing people and then redistributing that wealth for, let say, state-funded (i.e., tax-payer-funded) abortion. Funded abortion, indeed abortion itself, would go against the clear teaching of the Christian Bible, e.g., "You shall not murder."

Nor is it talking about state- (or taxpayer) funded education, whereby our children are to be sent to school for seven years or more to be taught by

Humanist educators where God hardly gets a foot in the door and Darwinism poses as true science. For this also would be to go against the clear teaching of Scripture, e.g., "Train up the child in the way that he should go and when he is older he will not depart from it." Why have so many departed from the Christian faith? State education has a lot to do with it…

Next, notice that these believers "had everything in common." Is this verse of Scripture to be the basis for Christians to excuse and even endorse the setting up a permanent program of government redistribution of wealth, i.e., Socialism/Communism?

A man greatly used by God to influence the progress of prosperity of Western Civilization was John Calvin. He answers this where he says the following about this verse,

> They brought forth and made common their goods in no other respect, save only that they might relieve the present necessity.[87]

As Calvin says, it was a *present* necessity. This was the time when the Church was transitioning from Old Testament (or Covenant) times to New Testament (or Covenant) times.

The Church, i.e., the body of believers, still takes up a collection every Sunday when it gathers for worship. But does the community of believers still have "everything in common"? Of course not! Some are richer. Some are poorer. But all give as they are

---

[87] John Calvin, *Calvin's Commentaries*, (Associated Publishers and Authors, Wilmington, Delaware, no date), 980.

able. Do you remember "The Widow's Mite" parable? She gave what she was able.

None of this for a moment suggests that the government should start dipping its hand into the pockets of its citizens, taking from this one or that group to give to this or that group! Their possessions are their own *private property*, to do with as they like, just as it was in the Church that this verse is referring to. Speaking of the same time Scripture says, "Then Peter said, 'Ananias, how is it that Satan has so filled your heart that you have lied to the Holy Spirit and have kept for yourself some of the money you received for the land? Didn't it belong to you before it was sold? And after it was sold, wasn't the money at your disposal?'" Acts 5:3-4a. What belonged to Ananias before he sold the land belonged to Ananias after he sold the land. It was his land and it was his money to do with as he pleased. It didn't belong to the Church. Nor did it belong to the government. It belonged to Ananias! Thus, the Bible teaches the principle of private property, which is anathema to Socialism and its intended goal, Communism.

JA Alexander, referring to this verse about Ananias, says,

> This shows conclusively, that no compulsory abandonment of property, or absolute community of goods, existed in the primitive church.[88]

---

[88] J.A. Alexander, *Acts: The Geneva Series of Commentaries*, (The Banner of Truth Trust, Reprinted 1984, Edinburgh), 190.

Yes, "All the believers were together and had everything in common", but when Howard Marshall comments on it, he says,

> We have avoided the use of the term 'communism' in describing this practice, since modern communism is a description of a political and economic system of such a different character that it is anachronistic and misleading to use the term in the present context.[89]

Says Rousas John Rushdoony,

> It is the custom among ecclesiastical socialists to deny that there is Biblical warrant for private property. Their ground for this is the often repeated Biblical declaration, "This earth is the LORD'S" (Ex. 9:29, etc.). They choose to neglect the total witness of Scripture to private property. The so-called communism of Acts 2:41-47, also cited by ecclesiastical socialists, was simply a voluntary sharing on the part of some (Acts 5). It was limited to Jerusalem. Because the believers took literally the words of Christ concerning the fall of Jerusalem (Matt. 24:1-28), they liquidated their properties there. The wealthier members placed some or all of these funds at the church's disposal, so that a witness could be made to their friends or

---

[89] Howard I. Marshall, *The Acts of the Apostles,* (Tyndale New Testament Commentaries, Eerdmans Publishing Company, Grand Rapids, Michigan, 1980), 84-85.

relatives before Jerusalem fell. Very early, persecution drove all but a nucleus out of Jerusalem (Acts 8:1).

The earth is indeed the Lord's, as is all dominion, but God has chosen to give dominion over the earth to man, subject to His law-word, and property is a central aspect of dominion. The absolute and transcendental title to property is the Lord's; the present and historical title is man's.[90]

It is astounding that some Christians have been duped into using this verse ("All the believers were together and had everything in common") to promote Socialism, when Socialism is an usurping and destructive intruder into Western Civilization and its healthy progress. Socialism is nothing but an anti-Christian overthrow of our Gospel freedoms. Says Rita Panahi,

Let's be honest here, Socialism is not about helping the poor but punishing the rich and using force to do so.[91]

Meanwhile still back in Scotland and to the Bible...

---

[90] Rousas John Rushdoony, *The Institutes of Biblical Law*, (The Presbyterian and Reformed Publishing Company, The Craig Press, 1973), 450-51.
[91] Rita Panahi, *The Outsiders*, Sky News, 10 February 2019.

Hidden Talents

I was having a bit of a laugh while reading some of the social media posts on a site pertaining to where I grew up in Scotland. Back in the day, there was an area of private housing that the locals referred to as "Spam Valley". Though some gave other reasons, apparently many of the locals called it that because some of the people who lived there, while struggling to pay mortgages beyond their means, could only afford to dine on cheap spam!

Spam was essentially the same thing as Klik in Canada, and is right up there with hot dogs, wieners, and internet spam for nutritional value. The Monty Python crew did a skit and even wrote a song about spam back in 1970!

What's wrong with eating spam? More to the point, what's wrong with making sacrifices in order to get ahead in life? According to the Bible, nothing! Pork and pork products had been put back on the Biblical menu with the advent of Jesus and the dissolution of Old Testament Israel. Speaking of Old Testament Israel as a body politic, under the heading, The Law of God, in chapter 19 of the Westminster Confession of Faith, we read the following as to what the Bible teaches about why many of the Old Testament laws, including dietary, have been rescinded:

> IV. To them also, as a body politic, he gave sundry judicial laws, which expired together with the state of that people, not obliging any other, now, further than the general equity thereof may require.

The Lord commanded Peter in a vision to kill and eat from a sheet full of unclean animals which was lowered to him from heaven. Peter was told, "What God has cleansed you must not call common" Acts 10:15b. This is one of the verses that Christians use to illustrate the expiration of Old Testament Israel as a body politic. It is a sad thing, but by pointing to what they think are contradictions in the Bible, (such as where a lot of Old Testament dietary laws, and laws about not wearing two different types of material, or sowing different types of seed together etc.), some think that they have an excuse to safely ignore God and His Word. And why would Socialism, whose whole system is based on government theft, want to have anything to do with the Bible anyway?

I don't know if envy, socialistic influence, or both were at the back of the somewhat disparaging title of "Spam Valley". Probably it was just meant to be humorous. However, contrary to Socialism, there is nothing wrong with owning a private home, as in owning private property. How do we know? Because the Bible teaches so. RC Sproul Jnr. well sums up the Bible's attitude to private property where he says,

> Ownership of property is sanctioned by God, from the garden paradise to Abraham's flock to the Promised Land to Saint Paul's tents.[92]

Take Jesus's Parable of the Talents in Matthew 25. Jesus tells the story of a rich businessman who was

---

[92] RC Sproul Jnr., *Dollar Signs of the Times-A Commonsense Guide to Securing Our Economic Future*, (Baker Books, Grand Rapids, Michigan, 1994), 18.

going overseas. He placed his business in the hands of his servants. (A "talent' is a weight measure, Revelation 16:21. Here it refers to cold hard cash, though, by way of extension, it may also by general equity or general principle be applied to gifts and talents).

Some employees were given more talents to play with than others, but all were expected to invest them with bankers and what have you, and thereby make lots of dosh before the businessman returned. We're talking millions of dollars here! This they all did, except for the one who buried the cash somewhere.

The businessman later returned, and generously rewarded each of his investors accordingly for their entrepreneurial diligence. However, the businessman was not happy with the "Socialist", the one who did not believe in Capitalism, i.e., the one who had hidden his talent. To him he said,

> You wicked and lazy servant, you knew that I reap where I have not sown, and gather where I have not scattered seed. So you ought to have deposited my money with the bankers, and at my coming I would have received back my own with interest. So take the talent from him, and give it to him who has ten talents. 'For to everyone who has, more will be given, and he will have abundance; but from him who does not have, even what he has will be taken away. And cast the unprofitable servant into the outer darkness. There will be weeping and gnashing of teeth' Matthew 25:26-30.

Of course, this is not to infer that every Socialist will be cast by Jesus on Judgment Day into "the outer darkness". There are some misguided Christians who think that the Bible actually teaches Socialism! My book, among other things, is my attempt to unteach that false teaching.

Socialism only encourages us to hide our God-given talents. Why invest your talents (as Jesus teaches us to) when a Socialist government, instead of rewarding you, is going to plunder your initial earnings with income tax and then your investments with a capital gains tax and then punish you some more with other taxes if you earn beyond some arbitrary amount set by government? This is unbiblical!

It is said glibly that Capitalism is a system built on exploitation and greed. That may be how misguided Socialists view Capitalism, however, as we have seen even by the brief allusion to Jesus's Parable of the Talents, clearly this is not God's view. To be sure, this is not to suggest that *some* Capitalists have not been exploitative and greedy. We're sure examples of such could be multiplied. However, the bottom line is that *all* Socialist governments are exploitative and greedy, especially when it comes to the rich and the financially successful.

While commenting on The Parable of the Talents, says the Bible commentator William Hendriksen,

> In passing, a safe inference would seem to be that Jesus, who tells this parable, is not opposed to responsible capitalism. Profit promotes

employment and makes possible helping those in need etc.[93]

I remember returning to Scotland from Canada in the 70s for a few months to convalesce after a serious operation. I noticed that there didn't seem to be any pizza delivery (as was ubiquitous in Toronto back then) taking place in my hometown. I should have got in there early and made my million organising "Uber Eats" before everyone and their West Highland Terrier dog got in on the act.

Also, I was too slow in opening up the car muffler repair business idea that I wanted to capitalise on. Alas! Apparently, a man who had spent some years in America, took the idea of specialising only in car silencers back to Edinburgh years ago with him and is now still laughing all the way to the bank! Well done him! My excuse is that, to begin with, I didn't have the initial capital to invest. Also, my plan was to live in Canada, not Scotland.

Now that I am living in sunny Australia, one of my entrepreneurial ideas is to capitalise on the novelty kopi luwak coffee, where people are willing to part with big bucks for a coffee, the beans of which, before being ground, have been defecated by a cat-like creature known as the Asian palm civet (Paradoxurus hermaphroditus)!

The Australian version of civet coffee could be kangaroo coffee, koala coffee, or kookaburra coffee. All I need is a coffee plantation and some iconic Australian critter that can eat and excrete partially

---

[93] William Hendriksen, *New Testament Commentary Matthew*, (The Banner of Truth Trust, Edinburgh, Reprinted 1976), 883.

digested coffee cherries! But don't hold your breath or send me any begging letters just yet…

Meanwhile back to the Bible…

Taxes & Taxation

The following numbered headings and accompanying comments have been designed to initiate (and hopefully stimulate) discussion on the question of taxes and taxation. The footnotes are given simply to include the thoughts and opinions of some fairly well-known Christians and Christian documents on some of the matters raised.

"The earth is the LORD'S, and all its fullness…" Psalm 24:1a. Since God owns everything, it is He who ought to be honoured for any (material) increase we receive. Therefore God's Word needs to be searched and consulted if Christians and Christianised societies (e.g., Western nations) are ever to be obedient to our God in such matters as tax and taxation. So, *"To the law and to the testimony!"*

1. *Is government taxation lawful?*

A question very much like this was asked of Jesus. "Is it lawful to pay taxes to Caesar, or not?" (We believe the tax referred to here was a Poll Tax upon the head of every male over the age of twenty years). Jesus replied, "Render therefore to Caesar the things that are Caesar's, and to God the things that are God's" Matthew 22:21. Therefore according to Jesus government taxation is lawful. David Chilton says,

The Bible does, of course, allow for some government taxation, but not much. The specific *form* of taxation (head tax, income tax, or whatever) is relatively unimportant, and is not set forth in Scripture; what *is* important is the *rate* of taxation, which determines the size of the state. As an absolute, outside limit, any tax of ten percent or more is specifically regarded by Scripture as *tyranny* – an attempt by rulers to be like God, extracting a 'tithe' (1 Samuel 8:15, 17).[94]

2. *Is government itself lawful?*

Again, Jesus in His "Render therefore to Caesar" answer legitimatised Civil Government, including government of a non-Christian kind. His Apostle who also lived under a pagan Roman government says, "Let every soul be subject to the governing authorities. For there is no governing authority except from God, and the authorities that exist are appointed by God" Romans 13:1. Government or Civil Magistracy is therefore lawful because it is God appointed.

The reason God has appointed the Magistrate is for the promotion of the doing of good works and the punishment of those who practice evil. The Apostle goes on to say, "For because of this you also pay taxes, for they are God's ministers attending continually to this very thing. Render therefore to all their due, taxes to whom taxes are due" (Romans 13:6-7a).

The compilers of the 1647 Westminster Confession of Faith (which is subscribed to by today's

---

[94] David Chilton, *Productive Christians, in an Age of Guilt Manipulators*, (Institute for Christian Economics, Tyler, Texas, 1981, Fourth Printing, April, 1986), 42.

Presbyterian Elders, whether Teaching Elders or Ruling Elders) are given the exalted title of the Westminster Divines, and these men say in the Confession,

> It is the duty of people to pray for magistrates, to honour their persons, to pay them tribute and other dues, to obey their lawful commands, and to be subject to their authority for conscience' sake. Infidelity, or difference in religion, doth not make void the magistrate's just and legal authority, nor free the people from their due obedience to him, from which ecclesiastical persons are not exempted.[95]

3. *Separation of Church and State?*

Does Jesus' statement about giving to Caesar what is Caesar's and to God what is God's suggest that paying taxes to the State has nothing to do with obedience to God? In other words, does Jesus here view the State as secular (as in having nothing to do with God?) Of course not!

The once upon a time Prime Minister of the Netherlands, Abraham Kuyper Snr., says,

> The sphere of the state itself stands under the majesty of the Lord. In that sphere there an independent responsibility to God is to be maintained. The sphere of the state is not profane. But both church and state must, each

---

[95] Westminster Confession of Faith XXIII:IV.

in its own sphere, obey God and serve His honor.[96]

The State is God's minister in the *civil* affairs of men, but not in *ecclesiastical* affairs (though it should also obediently promote the church's wellbeing by such things as tax-exemptions etc.) The word "separate" is too strong a word and has led to the idea of the separation of State and God! Therefore, though Church and State must remain distinct (rather than "separate"!) as functioning entities both are components of one nation under God.

RJ Rushdoony says,

> The nature of Israel's civil order [i.e., as per the Bible] is that God as King of Israel ruled from His throne room in the tabernacle, and to Him were the taxes brought. Because of the common error of viewing the tabernacle as an exclusively or essentially "religious," i.e., *ecclesiastical* center, there is a failure to recognize that it was indeed a *religious, civil* center. In terms of Biblical law, the state, home, school, and every other agency must be no less religious than the church. The sanctuary was thus the civil center of Israel and no less religious for that fact.[97]

---

[96] Abraham Kuyper, *Christianity As A Life-System-The Witness of a World-View*, (Christian Studies Center, America, 1980), 37.
[97] Rousas John Rushdoony, *The Institutes of Biblical Law*, Volume I, (The Presbyterian and Reformed Publishing Company, America, 1973), 281.

4. *Are Both Church and State Appointed by God?*

Magistrates and Governors are appointed by God for the good of society.[98] The Apostle Paul says to Titus, "Remind them to be subject to rulers and authorities, to obey, to be ready for every good work" (Titus 3:1). Jesus says, "On this rock I will build My church, and the gates of Hades shall not prevail against it" Matthew 16:18b. Therefore, since both Church and State have been appointed or established by God, and are under His authority, one would expect these bodies therefore to "reflect" something of the Godhead. Hence we see Church and State members paying tributes (i.e., tithes and taxes). These bodies in turn look after the peace and welfare of the many. Francis Nigel Lee says,

> The Church-of-the-future will need to set out, also in the various inter-relationships of human society — the full implications of the Father's paternity, the Son's filiation, and the Spirit's procession. For the Church needs to distinguish the various personal attributes of the Deity ontically (within Himself) — from their application economically (within man's world).[99]

---

[98] Abraham Kuyper says, "God has instituted the magistrates by reason of sin." *Christianity As A Life-System-The Witness of a World-View*, (Christian Studies Center, America, 1980), 28.

[99] Francis Nigel Lee, *God Triune In the Beginning – And For the 21ˢᵗ Century*, 3.

Since both are God ordained, our con-tributing tithes and taxes to Church and State is simply part of our religious obedience to the triune God.

5. *Is there a "principle" of taxation to be derived from intra-Trinitarian dealings?*

God is Triune. He is the One and the Many. Francis Nigel Lee says,

> The Three Persons within God Triune Himself, interpenetrate and overlap one another — which is quite what one would expect creatures of God Triune to do. Indeed, this is what Rev. Prof. Dr. Cornelius Van Til meant by "the one and the many." 1 Cor. 12:12-20.[100]

Therefore, as such, each Member of the Trinity con-tributes (voluntarily) *from His own distinct property,* to the Godhead. Therefore, "the Many" – each from His own increase and abundance – "pays tribute" to "the One". These "tributes" include Fatherliness, Sonship, and love, honour, respect, and gratitude, etc., for each of the Others. Thus the eternal peace, and the eternal welfare, of the many is perpetually maintained and sustained by the "One" through the (voluntary) con-tribution of the "Many."

6. *How Much Tax Should We Pay?*

Neither Church nor State is God. God alone is God. Therefore, we ought voluntarily to contribute our tithes and taxes because we want to be obedient to God in both these spheres. RC Sproul Jnr. says,

---

[100] Francis Nigel Lee, *ibid.,* 1.

Old Testament Israel had a system of not one tithe, but three. The first tithe went to the Levites… [who] were not just official priests, they were also teachers, musicians, judges, and physicians. Most of the tithe, in fact, went to those who were not priests. This illustrates a principle for today: all of our tithe need not go directly to the church; other institutions need our financial support too. It may go to a Christian educational organization, a Christian hospital, or Christian missions… The second tithe… was used for a yearly festival gathering…Deut. 14:26… The third tithe was not annual, but was offered in the third and sixth years of every seven-year-cycle…known as the poor tithe…Deut. 14:20-29.[101]

Therefore the foundational reason for *all* our giving must be the glory of God.

Early in the Bible it records men *giving of their increase* to God. Cain and Abel (voluntarily) brought *offerings of their increase* to God (Genesis 4:3-4). How much? We do not know. Abraham *gave a tithe* of all his increase of goods to Melchizedek the king of Salem and priest of God Most High (Genesis 14:20). Melchizedek was a Priest of God <u>and</u> the ruler of (the State) of Salem. Therefore, (though this is rather embryonic) Abraham (voluntarily) *gave a tenth of his increase to both religious spheres of Church and State.*

---

[101] RC Sproul Jnr., *Dollar Signs of the Times-A Commonsense Guide to Securing Our Economic Future*, (Baker Books, Grand Rapids, Michigan, 1994), 108.

Abraham's grandson Jacob demonstrates also a willingness *to pay at least ten percent of all his increase* to God (Genesis 28:22). It should be noted that Jacob's ten percent was commensurate with the increase of his goods as God prospered him. Taking, then, Abraham and Jacob as setting the Biblical precedent for (voluntary) giving, a maximum of ten percent of our income would be the fair contribution.

7. *On What Should We be Required to Pay Tax?*

We are to tithe and pay tax to God out of our increase, which is to say that we ought also to pay government *income tax*. If we pay the State income tax, then, our tithe to the Church must come from our net earnings, not our gross. Surely then, Church tithes should be tax-exempt! State taxes, like Church tithes, ought to be based *only* on income. Property tax is not a Biblical norm. RJ Rushdoony says,

> In the biblical law, the state has no right of eminent domain, and no right to tax the land. "It was impossible to dispossess men of their inheritance under the law of the Lord as no taxes were levied against land." The tithe was God's tax, not a gift to God. The state was limited to a tax resembling the tithe, a tax on increase, not on the land itself.[102]

Neither are the Goods and Services Tax (GST) and the Value Added Tax (VAT) the Biblical norm!

---

[102] Rousas John Rushdoony, *The Politics of Guilt and Pity*, (Thoburn Press, Fairfax, Virginia, 1978), 326.

However, Poll Taxes or Head Taxes are always Biblical (but are certainly not always popular!)

8. *Summary*
- God's Word must be the blueprint for all taxes and taxation
- Jesus Christ says that we are to "render unto Caesar". Therefore, we ought to pay taxes.
- Governments or Civil Authorities are "lawful" because they are appointed by God
- Though Church and State are distinct, both are to be honoured as legitimate spheres of Christian religion
- The principle of taxation may be derived from studying the Doctrine of the Trinity
- The principle of paying ten percent of our income is Biblical
- Our Church tithes and State taxes are to be paid *only* from our increase, i.e., income, but *not* on our property.

Much more could have been written above. However, it is hoped that the Christian's whistle has been sufficiently whetted so that he/she will now have a greater desire to search the Scriptures to see what more has been revealed therein about taxes and taxation.

For further study see, for example:
Money, goods or labour paid to a government as:
- Derived from people's possessions: 1 Sam. 8:10-18
- Derived from the poor: Amos 5:11

- Paid by forced labour: Deut. 20:11; 1 Kings 5:13-17
- Paid by foreigners: 1 Chron. 22:2
- Paid by all people: 2 Sam. 8:6;14
- Paid by all except Levites: Ezra 7:24
- Paid by Christians: Rom. 13:6,7

Taxes:
- Used for Sanctuary: Exo. 30:11-16
- Used for the king's household: 1 Kings 4:7-19

Meanwhile still on the subject of taxes…

Paying Taxes

'Then they sent to Him some of the Pharisees and the Herodians, to catch Him in His words. When they had come, they said to Him, "Teacher, we know that You are true, and care about no one; for You do not regard the person of men, but teach the way of God in truth. Is it lawful to pay taxes to Caesar, or not? Shall we pay, or shall we not pay?" But He, knowing their hypocrisy, said to them, "Why do you test Me? Bring Me a denarius that I may see it." So they brought it. And He said to them, "Whose image and inscription is this?" They said to Him, "Caesar's. And Jesus answered and said to them, "Render to Caesar the things that are Caesar's, and to God the things that are God's." And they marveled at Him' Mark 12:13-17.*

Speaking of taxes, taxes have been around for as long as governments. Now, the reasonable man doesn't mind paying his fair-share of tax. I mean, we all like to drive on decent roads. We all like to have our garbage picked up and dumped for us. We like to have the shores of our great nation defended against would-be invaders. Taxes are a necessary part of life for any ordered civilization.

We see that things were no different 2,000+ years ago in Palestine. The people at the time of Jesus, like us, had to pay taxes. We see (above in Mark 12:13-17) some sneaky people try to trick Jesus on the subject of taxes. Let me explain to you who these tricksters are. They are Pharisees and Herodians. They were sent by the chief priests, scribes, and elders mentioned back in Mark 11:27.

Now, before we get going, let's note that the Pharisees and Herodians disliked each other, intensely! However, here they are together, conspiring against a common enemy – Jesus Christ.

Most of us know the Pharisees as the hyper-legalistic religious sect which was dominating Israel at the time of Jesus. They were the ultra-nationalists of Israel, and they disliked intensely the Roman occupation of Palestine. The Herodians? Well, we don't know a great deal about the Herodians. The Herodians probably got their name from Herod the Great, who had received governorship of the kingdom of Judea by appointment of the Romans. The Herodians seem to have been affiliated with the Sadducees.

The Sadducees were the religious *liberals* of the day. The Herodians seem to be something like the *political wing* of the Sadducee sect. Albert Barnes says,

But here they are, the Pharisees who didn't favour Caesar, and the Herodians who did favour Caesar, in *cahoots* one with the other. So they toddle off to confront Jesus with a question about paying taxes.

Poll Tax

Every adult male in the whole of Judea had to pay a poll-tax. According to the historians this poll-tax came in around AD6 after Archelaus was deposed. Archelaus, who was the son of Herod, gets a mention in Matthew 2:22. Archelaus became ruler upon the death of his father Herod, but the Romans deposed him for misgovernment in AD6. Anyway, that's when this poll-tax or head-tax was introduced. So, the people of Judea had seen these taxes for some twenty-odd years.

Now, a number of years ago the British Government brought in a poll-tax in Scotland. After it was implemented in Scotland for about a year, the government introduced it into England. There were riots in the English streets! So the government of the day got the message and scrapped it. But not so with the Roman Government in Palestine. But anyhow, it's a poll-tax that's being referred to here in our text. RJ Rushdoony says,

---

[103] Albert Barnes, *Barnes' Notes on the New Testament*, (Kregel Publications, Grand Rapids, Michigan, 1982), 104.

The Herodians favored the Roman tax and the Herodian dynasty, which they regarded as preferable to direct Roman rule.[104]

The Herodians then, generally speaking, are pro-Roman government whereas the Pharisees are anti-Roman government. So, united and slimy they slide, slither and sidle up to Jesus and try to butter Him up. They patronize Jesus by telling Him that He teaches rightly, teaching the truth of God (Mark 12:14). They told Him that He doesn't show personal favouritism, either to the Pharisees or the Herodians. So, after they think they've done a good job of greasing Jesus up, they then slip in the question, "Is it lawful to pay taxes to Caesar, or not?"

You can see what they're trying to do here. They don't want to give Jesus any room to manoeuvre. "Is it right to pay the poll-tax – *Yes* or *No*?" So, keep in mind that you've got Pharisees and Herodians here. If Jesus said "Yes!" He'd appear to be siding with the Herodians and against His own people. And the Pharisees would immediately make sure everyone knew. And if Jesus said "No!" then the Herodians would make sure the Romans knew.

Is He going to show favouritism to the Pharisees and their cause or the Herodians and their cause? So, you can see the slight-of-hand going on here, can't you? Well, so could Jesus! Say "Yes" and He would be accused of showing *personal favouritism* toward the Herodians. Say "No" and He'd be accused

---

[104] Rousas John Rushdoony, *The Institutes of Biblical Law*, Volume I, "The Tribute Money", (The Presbyterian and Reformed Publishing Company, America, 1973), 718.

of showing *personal favouritism* toward the Pharisees. But as the Proverb says, "Surely, in vain the net is spread in the sight of any bird" 1:17.

Jesus being Jesus saw right through their little scheme.

Let me paint into the picture a little more of the historical background of what's going down here. The question they asked is this, "Is it lawful to pay taxes to Caesar, or not?" Now, I want to pick up on that word "lawful" – is it "lawful" or "right", as the NIV would have it. The same Greek word is used by the Pharisees, e.g., in Luke 6:1. There, Jesus and His disciples were walking through a grain field on the Sabbath. They were picking heads of grain and rubbed them in their hands as they walked. Some Pharisees said to them, "Why are you doing what is not <u>LAWFUL</u> on the Sabbath?" The Pharisees, as you know, had their own view of what was lawful, of what was right and wrong. They were forever distorting the Law of God, the measure of all that is right and wrong.

Jesus' "Sermon on the Mount" is one long correction of the Pharisees' mutilation of right and wrong. But here they are again, teamed up with the Herodians, trying to trick Jesus. And they believe that the poll-tax is wrong, unlawful. They see it as a form of slavery! Therefore if Jesus says it is lawful, they will instantly declare Him as the enemy of Israel!

There was a time when the people physically revolted against this tax. Luke in Acts 5:37 records these words in which Gamaliel, a Pharisee, says, "Judas of Galilee rose up in the days of the census, *[in the days of the taxing, KJV]* and drew away many people after him." Judas of Galilee led a revolt against the Romans in 6 or 7AD. The revolt against the Romans took place shortly after the poll-tax was introduced. And, according to Josephus the Historian, Judas of Galilee died in this revolt. According to Josephus, Judas of Galilee vehemently proclaimed, "Taxation is no better than downright slavery!" He saw this poll-tax as nothing less than treason against God! So, that's where the Pharisees are coming from in asking Jesus, "Is it lawful?" They're of the opinion of Judas of Galilee that it's most UN-lawful. And, of course, the Herodians were of the opinion that the poll-tax was lawful. So, who is right? The religious Legalists or the religious Liberals?

Now, just before we study the brilliant answer Jesus gave to that question, let's paint in some more detail into the backdrop. What you have here in the text is more similar to Australia (and the other Western nations) today than first meets the eye. The people of God, Israel, the Church, our Christian forefathers were then living among pagans. The non-Christians had the upperhand in all the realms of government. And *if* there was any Church representation on a government level, it was the Herodian/Sadducees, the religious (theological) liberals who were doing the representing. Is it any different today with the Church in Australia (and elsewhere)? Isn't it always the religious liberals with all their purple robes and gold crosses who represent the Church to the government? And where are the religious legalists today? Well, they're usually off forming their own <u>exclusive</u> denomination somewhere! And usually, like the Pharisees in Jesus' day, they tend to view any Christian entering politics as siding with the enemy. In other words, they view the government of the land and everything to do with it, even taxes, as the enemy!

Now, with all this in mind, the question before us becomes three-dimensional. To draw three dimensions on a piece of paper you need the length, breadth and height of the object. The object lesson we're trying to draw is about paying taxes. The Herodians, the religious liberals of Jesus' day, and the legalistic Pharisees argued over the length and breadth of the poll-tax. The Herodians had the extremely broad view and the Pharisees had the extremely narrow view. The Herodians had the length way too long and the Pharisees had the breadth far too narrow. But Jesus, Wisdom Incarnate, draws a three-dimensional picture for them. And He does this by bringing into the equation the missing point of reference, i.e., God! How did He do it? Well, He asks them to show Him a denarius, the coin used to pay the poll-tax. Then He gets them to have a look at it, "Whose image, whose "icon" is this?" Mark 12:16. "And whose signature, whose 'epigraph' inscription is on it? They answered and said, 'Caesar's'" Then Jesus gives them His brilliant answer, "Render therefore to Caesar the things that are Caesar's, and to God the things that are God's." Or in the NMV, i.e., the Neil McKinlay Version, "Pay Caesar the Poll-Tax <u>AND</u> pay God the Soul-Tax!"

So Jesus, contrary to the opinion of the Pharisees stated that it is lawful to pay taxes to Caesar. But He shows them that not only is there a tax on their head, but also on their soul! So let's move on to our second point as I explain the soul tax.

Jesus answered the question, "Is it lawful to pay taxes to Caesar?" in the affirmative. I hope you can see that, for it's very important that you see it. Taxes, and we're talking about "lawful" taxes, are a necessary part of life. It's the teaching of Jesus, which is the teaching of Scripture. E.g., after explaining what the Civil Government is for, Paul the Apostle says in Romans 13:6-7, "For because of this you also pay taxes, for they [i.e., the government] are God's ministers attending continually to this very thing. Render therefore to all their due: taxes to whom taxes are due..." etc. So then, we've to render to *all* their due. We've to render Caesar, or the Civil Government of our day, their due. And also we've to render to God His due.

Now, some people have a great amount of difficulty seeing the connection between rendering unto Caesar and rendering unto God. We have concluded in light of the Scriptural teaching of Jesus that paying taxes is lawful. That even paying taxes to the pagan Roman Government was lawful, it was right. Therefore, not to pay taxes, as in being a tax-dodger, would be unlawful. It would be wrong. It would make you a law-breaker.

I know someone who refused to pay the government Poll-tax when it was brought in for that year in Scotland. He was even willing to go to jail on principle. However, he subsequently decided to pay back to the government every penny he owed. Why? Because he loves paying taxes? Who does? He's paid back every penny because of the grace of God. You see, God by His grace and mercy had converted him since that time. So, he wanted to gratefully serve his Saviour by being obedient to Him, even in paying taxes!

Can't you see that paying taxes is being obedient to God? Or are you one of those who detaches God from the world? Do you think that this world belongs to Satan and so do all Governments on earth? Well, why would Jesus tell you to pay your taxes to the Devil and his Government minions? No, you need to see that all Government bodies on earth are *as* accountable to God *as* are you and I! Romans 13:1-2, "Let every soul be subject to the governing authorities. For there is no authority except from God, and the authorities that exist are appointed by God. Therefore whoever resists the authority resists the ordinance of God, and those who resist will bring judgment on themselves."

Caesar was only a man, the figurehead of the Roman Government in Jesus' day. It was his image, his "icon", that was on the coin used for the poll-tax. And the idea that Jesus was conveying was, that since Caesar's image and signature was on the tax-coin, the coin <u>BELONGED</u> to him. It's like when we were kids, if you saw a coin on the ground and said, *"That's mine!"* someone was sure to say, *"Is your name on it?"* And if your name wasn't on it, you might have a fight over whose money it was! (Of course, technically, the money belonged to whoever had lost it. I merely illustrate a point.) However, Caesar's image and signature were on the Roman money, so it belonged to Caesar.

Now then, as we recap a little. We've seen that the Herodians and Pharisees tried to trick Jesus. But

Jesus sprung their plot by use of a *silver* coin with Caesar's image and signature on it. Jesus told them, because it had Caesar's image and signature on it, it therefore belonged to Caesar. Hence the words, "Render to Caesar the things that <u>ARE</u> Caesar's. And we've seen then, that this is the lawful thing to do. Therefore paying taxes is right!

Let me ask: What is man? Who or what are you and I? What does Jesus and the Scriptures teach about you and me? Whose *image* are we, and whose *inscription* is on us? We understand the Poll-tax, but what about the Soul-tax, have we really understood it? Have we really comprehended what it means to Render to God the things that are God's? Well, you need to understand that God owns you, God owns me, for He made us, He minted us! And the tax that He demands of you and me is that you love the LORD our God with all your heart, soul, strength and mind, and your neighbour as yourself.

Now, the mad and crazy and bizarre thing about this, is that there are people willing to go to prison forever, and suffer the torments of hell forever, rather than pay the Soul-tax! And, they want to do so on a matter of principle! They claim that God has no right to make any demands of them! They claim that it is not right, that it's unlawful to do so! Therefore they withhold their Soul-tax from God whose image they are. Some even want to form God in their own image. That's why there's any number of false gods around the world.

Some have formed a god they can treat as non-existent! However, the God who has revealed Himself propositionally in Scripture, the God who has revealed

Himself in His Son Jesus Christ may demand His Soul-tax of you this very day, and how are you going to make payment? Are you going to try to fob Him off with an old, bent, twisted, distorted and tarnished coin? I'm talking about you and me!

The image of God is so unrecognizable and the signature so illegible, that you and I are no longer legal tender in God's eyes. We're only fit to be melted down as so much scrap metal! But God by His grace and mercy, by His kindness has given us the necessary and required currency. He's given us what we need to escape the great *melt-down* on the Last Day that Peter speaks of, (see 2 Peter 3:10-13).

However, the Good News is, "For God so loved the world that He gave His only begotten Son, that whoever believes in Him should not perish but have everlasting life" John 3:16.

What the Soul-tax God demands of you is a perfect life, where every single thought, word and deed throughout your whole life from womb to tomb was unblemished! For this perfect life would be a reflection of the God who made you. For that's what it means to love God with all your heart, soul, strength and mind, and your neighbour as yourself. It's to reflect the Triune God. There's only ever been one Person who has done this since the Fall of man. And, if you don't already know Him, God is offering Him to you.

Even Caesar is to render unto God the things that are God's. We all are to.

Will you give up your Soul-tax evasion and receive the gift God is offering? God is offering you, free of charge, the Soul-tax that He demands of you! He is offering you His perfect Son who is the perfect, i.e., the express image of God. Jesus Christ has the signature, the name of God written on Him. He is the only legal tender in heaven. And the way to receive this gift of God is to recognize how tarnished you are as the image of God. Your thoughts are blemished, your words are stained, and your deeds are as filthy rags. Don't insult God by thinking you can offer yourself as the Soul-Tax payment. Acknowledge to God that you are illegal tender in His eyes.

As Jesus says in Mark 1:15, "The time is fulfilled, and the kingdom of God is at hand. Repent, and believe in the gospel."

If you haven't already, accept then the gift He has offered. Believe in Jesus Christ to save you. Trust in Jesus Christ *alone* as your Soul-Tax payment. If, by God's grace you do this, or if by God's grace you have done/are doing this, then God will welcome you into heaven. He will welcome you when He calls on you to make that final payment! But meanwhile, show your gratitude to God, do what your Saviour says – even when paying taxes. "Render to Caesar the things that are Caesar's, and to God the things that are God's."

Meanwhile back to the Bible (but on a different subject to taxes)…

Towards a Reconstructed Society

"Therefore I exhort first of all that… prayers… be made for kings and all who are in authority, that we may lead a quiet and peaceable life in all godliness and reverence. For this is good and acceptable in the sight of God our Saviour" 1 Timothy 2:1-3.

If Christians wish to demonstrate love for God and neighbour, then they ought to pray for the governing bodies having authority over them. For what hope do Christians have of living *quiet and peaceable lives in all godliness and reverence* if the civil authority is ungodly and irreverent in its use of its God ordained authority? Governing authorities exist to promote man's good and to execute wrath on practisers of evil (Romans 13:4).

This being said, it necessarily follows that we beg the question: By what standard? How ought the Civil Authority measure good and evil? After all he has the authority to use both the flat edge and the sharp edge of the sword of justice, as the case may require.

To put the question another way: What types of things ought Christians to pray for regarding these authorities whose existence is in order to promote good, restrain, and even punish evil?

Should the Christian expect non-Christian authorities to pass laws in accordance with God's immutable Moral Law (i.e., the Ten Commandments)? He should if the State Constitution the Civil Authority is under requires it. Says Joel McDurmon,

> The church should have the loudest voice when it comes to determining what is right or wrong in society. If laws or proposed laws do not line up with biblical law, the church should condemn them clearly.[105]

But what of those nations whose Constitution is not founded or based upon God's Law? What should

---

[105] Joel McDurmon, *God versus Socialism: A Biblical Critique of the New Social Gospel*, (American Vision Press, Powder Springs, Georgia, 2009), 100.

the Christian pray for then? Surely he or she should pray for the same as the former. Which is to say that Christians everywhere ought to pray that they *may lead quiet and peaceable lives in all godliness and reverence.* Therefore, Christians *need* to be under, and need to seek to be under, civil authorities that honour each of God's Ten Commandments.

Christians therefore must pray that the civil authorities will indeed promote good and punish evil *in accordance with God's Word.* For only *then* will peace and quiet be possible for Christians in any nation.

Speaking very generally, this was, to a certain extent, the case in most Westernised countries prior to the 1960s. Civil authorities in the West used to promote, for example, the Christian Sunday Sabbath (4th Commandment) by preventing department stores and the likes from opening, and keeping the pubs closed; and regulating the bar hours for that day in hotels etc.

Also, people were required to take oaths on the Bible (3rd & 9th Commandments); and respect those in authority such as parents, teachers, police, judges etc. (5th Commandment). Murderers, (6th Commandment) in many cases, received the death penalty; adultery (7th Commandment) was certainly frowned upon (and sometimes punished), theft (8th Commandment) was abhorred and punished accordingly, lying (9th Commandment) was likewise abhorred as shameful. New "citizens" of Western nations made their oath "under God" (1st Commandment). It would seem then, that only the 2nd and 10th (Graven Images and Coveting respectively) Commandments were not *openly* countenanced.

Interestingly, Roman Catholicism attempts to absorb the 2nd Commandment (the use of images) as part of, or an appendix to, the 1st Commandment (no God but God). And, in order to maintain the number of Commandments as the traditionally accepted ten, Rome divides the 10th (coveting) in two.

All in all, before the 60s, the governing authorities in the West generally stood on the solid ground of God's Law for promoting the good in society and punishing evildoers. With this in mind, Christians should pray that the civil authorities to whom they are subject will once again return (in the West) to the solid bedrock of God's Law and begin to wisely implement it.

But what if there are some who do not wish to come under the implementation of God's Law? What is there to guard their "civil liberties"? How is the governing authority to promote *their* good and punish *their* evil doing? To ask this question another way, should any one individual or group in society be exempted from keeping God's Law as properly administered and upheld by its lawful authorities? For example, what about the criminally insane? Should they be punished for their crimes? Are they even eligible to commit crimes? What about refugees? etc., etc.

Surely the answer to these and such like questions is that justice must remain blindfolded? Otherwise there will be no justice for all! After all, God's Law is God's Law for all; whether Jew, Mohammedan, Hindu, Atheist, Secularist, etc., even the criminally insane. Therefore the Christian must answer these and like questions in the affirmative. Yes, there should be no person or group above God's Law. Each must be held accountable for his own actions. Which is not to say that the infantile and the imbecilic are expected to comply to the same degree as the mature-minded. Hence special consideration needs to precede any punishment for their wrongdoing.

God's Word says that the Civil Authority receives his authority from God (Romans 13:1-7; John 19:10-11). Therefore "he is God's minister to you for good. But if you do evil, be afraid; for he does not bear the sword in vain; for he is God's minister, an avenger to execute wrath on him who practices evil" Romans 13:4. To be God's minister at law one must honour and strive to uphold God's Law, even when meting out due punishment. Says Joel McDurmon,

> In biblical thought, the State is a subordinate institution to God's law. This means, among other things, that the State cannot legislate beyond what Scripture warrants, nor can it use its monopoly of force in any area of society that Scripture keeps free. Thus the State cannot interfere with the sanctions of the church (baptism, discipline, and excommunication), nor the family (education, finance). The State exists to punish evil by ministering God's wrath. Going beyond this the State usurps the role of other divine institutions and even of God Himself.[106]

---

[106] Ibid., 99.

So, who goes to jail? Only those, who have broken God's Law, as it is read (interpreted?), and applied, by the civil authority for the good of society. But, more to the point, what is jail? Is jail not simply a secure holding place for those accused and awaiting *trial* for crimes? and also, for those awaiting *punishment* for their crime, such as murderers? Jail, itself, does not seem to be a biblical form of punishment for evildoers. Indeed, God Himself is keeping fallen angels "reserved in everlasting chains under darkness for the judgment of the great day…" Jude 6. Restitution or death are apparently the only two biblical options for guilty criminals.

Christians need to pray then for their Civil Authorities. Christ is building His kingdom from the inside out. Therefore Christians must also seek to evangelise their Civil Authorities so that their hearts might be changed by the power of the Gospel. Reconstructed hearts mean a reconstructed society.

Meanwhile still back to the Bible…

The West's Ancient Landmarks

"Do not remove the ancient landmark which your fathers have set" Proverbs 22:28. This verse, of course, refers to God's people upon their entrance into the Promised Land. In short, they were to honour their God-given inheritance by respecting each other's private property (cf. Duet. 19:14; 27:17; Job 24:2; Prov. 15:25). This, upon reflection, is merely an application of the 8th Commandment, which is, "You shall not steal" Exodus 20:15.

None of us would like it were our neighbour to move his boundary fence onto our property. It would be theft. He would be stealing what is rightfully and lawfully ours. The freedoms and economic prosperity we enjoy in the West have a great deal to do with the concept of private property or ownership as defined in the Bible. Boundaries are Biblical.

Before we look at the application of this Biblical principle we need to acknowledge that boundaries are grounded in the Triune God. The Father is not the Son or the Spirit. Nor is the Son the Father or the Spirit. Nor is the Spirit the Father or the Son. Though the three Persons in the Godhead are equal in substance, power, and eternity, "The LORD our God, the LORD is one" (Deuteronomy 6:4), each Person interpenetrates the Others. But each owns private property: Fatherhood, Sonship, and Spiritness.

The Ten Commandments collectively express the character of God. Each Commandment individually expresses some certain aspect of the God who has from all eternity loved God and His Neighbour as Himself in the eternal Triune Godhead. The Father does not try to steal sonship or spiritness. Nor does the Son wish to rob either the Father or the Spirit of Their private property. Nor does the Spirit wish to steal fatherhood from the Father or sonship from the Son. Thus each Person respects the "landmarks" within the Godhead.

God has written His Moral Law on the heart of every member of the human race (Rom. 2:14-15). This is what is known as the Law of Nature or Natural Law. This Moral Law was also written as the Ten Commandments. Because our nature is now fallen, the Law written on stone tablets (as revealed and expounded in Scripture) helps us to understand the Law written on fleshly tablets, i.e., our hearts.

Today we are witnessing a removal of many of the ancient and Biblical landmarks our fathers set in human society. Take the way the Revisionists have been busy rewriting and redefining history to suit their social engineering agenda in which all reference to the God of Christianity and even Christianity itself is removed from the Western nations in an attempt to transform it into their own image and likeness. Examples of this form of Political Correctness are legion. For example, in the USA there is now a grassroots movement rediscovering the *real* George Washington. Indeed, there is a renewed interest in rediscovering all of their founding fathers as they *actually* existed and not as they have been recreated in image of the revisionist.

For decades America's founding fathers, through sloppy scholarship (or perhaps something more ominous), have been portrayed in school textbooks as Deists at best or Atheists at worst! Yet, one only has to read their own writings (which are abundantly extant) to see that most were Bible believing Christians. Their God, the One they prayed to and worshiped and honoured in their writings, is the Triune God who has revealed Himself in Scripture. Scholars quoting other scholars do not make for accurate and dependable textbooks. Only by sourcing the original will we bypass their obvious biases.

The West's ancient landmark is the Bible. Ponder again the following words, "Do not remove the ancient landmark which your fathers have set" Proverbs 22:28.

Like those of the USA, the Legal Systems of the Commonwealth nations are based on the teaching of Scripture through the likes of Sir William Blackstone (1723-80), the Westminster Assembly (1643-52), the Declaration of Arbroath (1320), the Magna Carta (1215), King Alfred the Great (849-99), the early Church, all the way back to Moses and the Decalogue (B.C. 1400).

In the West, through its system of Common Law, the Ten Commandments are applied in the light of the Gospel, which is to say that, when required, justice is to be tempered with mercy. To be sure the West at times drifts away from its Biblical moorings. Social landmarks get shifted or removed as the tide ebbs and flows between political philosophies. Says Francis Nigel Lee, (who, among other things, was a qualified Barrister),

> The Biblical contribution to our notion of justice and legal consciousness has been widely acknowledged. Jurists see in the Biblical Scriptures one of the main foundations of Western civilization and the "rule of law."[107]

Under inspiration of the Spirit, the Psalmist says, "If the foundations are destroyed, What can the righteous do?" Psalm 11:3. Who would seek to destroy the foundations of Western Civilization? Who would wish to remove the ancient landmarks our fathers have set? My prayer is that it is not you.

Meanwhile still back to the Bible…

---

[107] Francis Nigel Lee, *Common Law: Roots and Fruits*, 92.

Bodies and Borders

Why do countries have borders? One might as well ask why humans have bodies. Both are because God created mankind to occupy specific geographical locations. Thus humans and countries are restricted by borders. To be sure, we expand our borders as individuals as our bodies increase from infancy to adulthood. But still, like nations, we are restricted by boundaries. We put on weight, we lose weight. And so the tide goes out, and the tide comes in on our nation. Those boundaries have been put there by God who made us. God alone has no boundaries.

Each member state of the European Union has an open border policy towards other member states. There is a free flow of people toing and froing. Then refugees (and others) started flooding in from African countries across the Mediterranean, i.e., non-member countries. As Chancellor of Germany, Angela Merkel opened up her country to an extraordinary amount of them, placing an onerous burden on the German tax-payer to support these newcomers. Same for Denmark and Sweden, and all the countries that opened their borders to the African nations, i.e., EU non-member states.

America has an extraordinary influx of people from Central and South American countries. Instead of applying to enter legally, these migrants simply cross the border. Like the illegal aliens flowing into Europe, these ("Undocumented Immigrants", as the Left likes to call them), place an extreme burden on the American tax-payer, especially in those states that run along the border with Mexico. Huge caravans of people arrive at the American border and demand to be let in.

President Donald Trump ran for election on promises to "build a wall". He struggles to get funding support from the Establishment politicians, not exclusively but especially those on the Left. In fact a member of The House of Representatives, Speaker of the House Nancy Pelosi has said, "Most of us, speaking for myself, consider the wall immoral, ineffective." We can handle her use of the word "ineffective', but "immoral"? How can a wall on the border of your country to keep out interlopers be immoral? Of course, we ought to have figured out already by the Left's use of the term "undocumented immigrants" instead of the term as it stands in the lawbooks, i.e., "illegal aliens", that the Democrats do not believe in borders. Those on the right say that this is because those "undocumented immigrants" are "undocumented Democrats"! Socialists always vote for the party that promises them free handouts. And so the tit for tat between Democrats and Republicans goes on and on.

Is a border wall immoral? We may as well ask: Are borders Biblical? The answer is, of course borders are Biblical. In case you miss it, if a thing is Biblical it cannot be immoral. How so? Because our morals come from God.

America, like Australia, takes in more than its fair share of immigrants. There is a legal process for entrance. Australia had to contend with countless illegals arriving on its shores in boats, many of them drowning at sea. Countless lives have been saved by Australia's "stop the boats" policy which worked to discourage people smugglers.

Borders are Biblical, even country borders that have walls, just as there was a wall around Jerusalem to protect its people from invasion.

Who knows how many angels can dance on the head of a pin, and why should we even care? But we do know that each angel and each collective host of angels, though not having material bodies, occupies restricted space. For God alone is omnipresent. Even the Devil can't be everywhere at once, having to go "to and fro on the earth" (Job 1:7). Same with those wicked angels who left their own abode to join him (Jude 6).

God has us all right where He wants us to be, and when He wants us to be. And even when we die we still occupy a restricted space individually and collectively. And, we won't escape from our bodies for long; for mankind's Resurrection Day is ahead (John 5:28-29).

Let's face it, as individuals we are as restricted by our bodies as countries are restricted by their borders. Is this such a bad thing? Not if you have groped for God and found Him. For Scripture says, "And He has made from one blood every nation of men to dwell on all the face of the earth, and has determined their preappointed times and the boundaries of their dwellings, so that they should seek the Lord, in the hope that they might grope for Him and find Him, though He is not far from each of us" Acts 17:26-27.

Individuals are to grope for God. Nations are to grope for God. Therefore individually and collectively we are to seek the God who made us of one blood in Adam.

It's a sad thing when a person closes himself to God. It is even sadder when a nation closes its borders to God. But the good news is that God has no boundaries! No heart of stone and no 'Iron' or 'Bamboo Curtain' can stop Almighty God entering should He wish.

As individuals we are to use our bodies to glorify God (1 Corinthians 6:10). Collectively, as a nation, we are to glorify God (Psalm 117:1). "Blessed is the nation whose God is the LORD, the people He has chosen for His own inheritance. The LORD looks from heaven; He sees the sons of men. From the place of His dwelling He looks on all the inhabitants of the earth; He fashions their hearts individually; He considers all their works" Psalm 33:12-15.

Why fade away and disappear as an individual? Why disappear as a nation? Open your heart and borders to the true and living Triune God who "… did not send His Son into the world to condemn the world, but that the world through Him might be saved" John 3:17.

The sovereign God has put you in your body and you in your nation. Therefore look only to God the Father, Son, and Holy Spirit if you would seek to extend your own, and your nation's, borders. Think outside your own body!

Meanwhile still back to the Bible (but a poetic and optimistic conclusion)…

Peace on Earth

Swords beaten into ploughshares, spears into pruning hooks the nations study war no more. In their pre-appointed times and within the boundaries of their dwellings the nations are many yet one under the doting eye of the Triune God – the original One and Many. In solemn league and covenant with each other and with God, the Bible (applied to their diverse situations), is their constitution and unity. God's law is their delight, meditated on day and night. On each nation's flag the words, "Love God and your neighbour as yourself."

Says Jehovah, "Now it shall come to pass in the latter days that the mountain of the LORD's house shall be established on the top of the mountains, and shall be exalted above the hills; and all nations shall flow to it" Isaiah 2:2.

As was the red cord of Rahab, so their nation's flag will be draped from a window of their own homes. Each person under their own fig tree meditates on things noble, just, pure, lovely, and virtuous – praiseworthy things, things of good report. Each season their vineyards and fruit trees give forth in abundance.

While receiving his sight a blind man once said, "I see men like trees, walking." The LORD says, "For as the days of a tree, so shall be the days of my people, and My elect shall long enjoy the work of their hands" Isaiah 65:22b. Like trees planted by rivers of waters, each brings forth fruit in its season. And written on each renewed heart is the Law of Love, the Ten Commandments. Age-wrinkles all but ironed out, the centenarian dies a young man! And, "the nursing child shall play by the cobra's hole, and the weaned child shall put his hand in the viper's den. They shall not hurt nor destroy in all My holy mountain, for the earth shall be full of the knowledge of the LORD as the waters cover the sea" Isaiah 11:8-9.

Christ's government began as a seed, the Seed of the Woman. The LORD said to the serpent Satan, "And I will put enmity between you and the woman, and between your seed and her Seed; He shall bruise your head, and you shall bruise His heel" Genesis 3:15. As the woman Jael swung the workman's hammer to pound a tent peg into the ground through Sisera's head, as "a certain woman dropped an upper millstone on Abimelech's head and crushed his skull," so the Woman's Seed crushed the serpent's head by the nails of His cross and the stone that rolled away.

Jehovah-Jesus says of Himself, "And whoever falls on this stone will be broken; but on whomever it falls, it will grind him to powder" Matthew 21:44. Christ is the Rock from which streams of living water flow. His kingdom is the stone that was cut out without hands crushing the image of all that exalts itself against the knowledge of God. "The stone that struck the image became a great mountain and filled the whole earth" Daniel 2:35b. Like the covering cherub cast out of Eden – the mountain of God – so will be all who oppose the spread of Christ's Gospel kingdom. "For unto us a Child is born, unto us a Son is given; and the government will be upon His shoulder. And His name will be called, Wonderful, Counsellor, Mighty God, Everlasting Father, Prince of Peace. Of the increase of His government and peace there will be no end, upon the throne of David and over His kingdom, to order it and establish it with judgment and justice from that time forward, even forever. The zeal of the LORD of hosts will perform this" Isaiah 9:6-7. *"Behold, the virgin shall be with child, and bear a Son, and they shall call His name Immanuel,* which is translated, "God with us" Matthew 1:23. At the birth of the Prince of Peace the angels said, "Glory to God in the highest, and on earth peace, goodwill toward men!" Luke 2:14. The thief on the cross said to Jesus, "Lord, remember me when You come into Your kingdom" Luke 23:42.

After His resurrection and coming into His kingdom Jehovah-Jesus met with His trained disciples on an appointed mountain, saying to them, "All authority has been given to Me in heaven and earth. Go therefore and make disciples of all the nations, baptizing them in the name of the Father and of the Son and of the Holy Spirit, teaching them to observe all things that I have commanded you; and lo, I am with you always, even to the end of the age" Matthew 28:18-20. Daniel takes up the story, "I was watching in the night visions, and behold, One like the Son of Man, coming with the clouds of heaven! He came to the Ancient of Days, and they brought Him near before Him. Then to Him was given dominion and glory and a kingdom, that all peoples, nations, and languages, should serve Him. His dominion is an everlasting dominion, which shall not pass away, and His kingdom the one which shall not be destroyed" Daniel 7:13-14.

Don't follow Marx. Follow Christ! Therefore, don't vote for any type of socialist government. Vote for Christ's government today!